METAMORPHOSIS

Copyright © 2024 by D. Hernandez

All rights reserved. No part of this book may be reproduced in any manner whatsoever. This includes graphic electronic, mechanical, including photocopying, recording, taping, or by any information storage retrieval system without written permission except in the case of brief quotations embodied in critical articles and reviews. No reordering of the poems are permitted for other publication.

First Printing, 2024

Contact ruben @ rdecwapub@gmail.com for copyright questions

This Christmas edition is dedicated to the people who raised me. Mainly because my mother still believes in Santa Clause and my father always found a way to get gifts under the tree. Even when we had next to nothing.

So much love for who y'all were.

Y'all means all.
So I have been told.

This collection of poems is dedicated to all the failed poets. Those counter cultural morons drunk on ideals that never quite fit the mold of reality. Those who refuse to be broken at the expense of being destroyed. It is the fate of us unbroken romantics.

This work ethic is dedicated to the day laborers I worked with.

This sense of inquiry is dedicated to my fellow philosophers.

This strength is dedicated to all the teachers putting in long hours.

This change I want to create is dedicated to all the students. You are whole and are inheriting a broken world. Not the other way around.

It goes without saying my love goes out to all of those living on the margins.

Siempre Adelante,

ruben

Introduction to the Christmas Edition

    I think putting out a Christmas edition provides a unique opportunity to make changes and additions. Though I will not be removing any of the original content besides the cover image.
    I have decided not to remove any of the interior despite some poems and arguable whole sections are just bad. My reason for doing this is quite simple. I have put these poems in chronological order. In the words of Joy Harjo, "Poetry is the map of the soul". I am the furthest thing from perfect, but I am a perfectionist (sorta) (it's unclear even to me). This trajectory of becoming the poet that I am has been jadded and confusing. There are many poems in this project do not adequately reflect who I am currently. The type of poet that I have become. And I chose to include them. I am choosing to keep them. Their imperfection is supposed to highlight my development as an artist. This project, in order to achieve it's maximum potential, breaks the traditional conventions of an artist's anthology. Where normally the inclination may be to open to a random page and see what speaks to you. Though I think that can still be a unique experience, the structural organization of this project is just as important the content itself. If you read it chronologically not only will you experience the development of my abilities, but you will bear witness to the maturation of my political and religious beliefs. You will also the transitions of me battling depression, solitude, and periods of my life in which I "struggled" with sobriety.

I cannot give you guys an autobiography though I feel the demand to write down all the adventures. The two reasons behind this is I generally struggle to write about myself in a direct way and my life story is still telling me what is happening. I can't tell you guys my autobiography because my life story is still happening.

With that being said I was never interested in fame despite this proclivity to put my self in the light of the spectacle. I write fiction because the author isn't there. The stories are the stories without me. The main reason I have written under pen names was to protect the sanctity of my privacy.

If you want a good autobiography, then you should implore my brothers to write something. They have lived equally exciting lives. Arguably more exciting. Or my cousisns. Or my parents. God knows they want the attention that I refuse. If they weren't too busy being who they are I would even be willing to help them become who they could be. I am sure they are saying the same thing about me.

I'll write my story once I leave the circus, but I am in the middle of my set.

In the words of Joy Harjo, "Poetry is the map of the soul". This project is intended to be read in chronological order. Which isn't the typical approach to poetry projects, but I became who I am through the poetic act. If you read it the way it is intended you will feel the transitions of my life as opposed to me telling you about what they were. These poems may not be your traditional autobiography, but they are the autobiography of my emotional and spiritual states.

That is why I am fairly confident that my editions of my work will do well long term compared to the supposed immediate success of my work being canabalized and being sold as seperate editions.

I will tell you one thing about who I am. It is a song lyric from one of my South American bands. La Vela Puerca. "No soy ningun profeta, soy simplement aguantador.". I am no prophet, I am a man who has endured many emberrasments.

IX | INTRODUCTION TO THE CHRISTMAS EDITION

I hope that perhaps this introduction will help contextualize the absurdity (bear in my mind that I am an absurd man) of the cover of the paperback edition of this project. "False Profit" was going to be the title of the project, but abusive and advantegous people purchased the copyrights to that title before I could finalize the details of my project. I had to call a last minute audible. "Metamorphosis" felt like the natural choice. It is the caption of my first instagram post on the profile dedicated to the "ruben" alias. It is also the title of Kafka's seminal work in which Samsa becomes a cockroach overnight. Without warning I too became a mighty cockroach.

Hear I was this Bukowski-esque idividual struggling with dependency (undeniably at a distance compared to those who have a better claim to such suffering), depression, and PTSD deemed a pious individual because I have a charitable soul, was writing poetry in public, and am ethnically ambigious. I don't think I speak about religiousness and spirituality more than the average individual in our time. But when the world feels like it is ending (no matter what era of humanity you live in it always feels like it is about to come apart) and I cannot deny the fact that my sophisticated hippie ass does look like the second coming---it seems somewhat inevitable that people might make assumptions that are not there. I would like to confirm that I am not in fact Jesus Christ.Nor am I Jesus Christ 2.0 with the newest and latest software update. I am no more the son of God then any other individual on this planet.

This assumption made by others feels somewhat ironic. Ironic because I am somewhat unholy. I am unholy because we live in unholy times and I am an artist. To do this shirt right you can't lean into the algorithm of what works. You gotta disrupt and I am a real disruptive mother fucker.

So, False Profit. A play on words. Poking fun at the assumptions made about my appearance and how starkly they contrasted the struggle fate has imposed upon my journey. Even a play onto how much I struggle to accept the presence of a higher power in my life. If there is anything about me that is remotely pious is my dedication to doing the right thing. To align myself with the truth even if it is at the expense of my reputation and relationships. It's a lonely life, but it's a damn good one.

Profit instead of prophet because of the ways my pocket's have been lined. Swiped. Gotten got. Hussled. I am happy people are reading my work. I am grateful that my work seems to be doing something. I am a ripple pushing currents. How can I not feel incredibly honored, but I cannot be your Marxist hero. I cannot be the great socialist of self sacrifice. I wish I was but this art thing---if you read this project the way it is intended it will be blatantly obvious---used to feel like gift and that was why I wanted to share it, but it's a foresaken plague. I am constantly narrating. I hear colors. I see music. When I am not creating I am barely holding myself together. I have to be the agent of change in my own life and I can't do that unless I have agency over my intellectual property.

But I had and have no idea who is this allusive pick pocket. It feels like I am shooting a gun into the sky and yelling, "Fight.". An incredibly irresponsible and reckless approach to justice, but I can't afford lawyers. I can't afford my bills. Maybe I am shooting a gun into the sky. That's one way to look at it. Another way to look at it is that I am abandoned at sea. Surrounded by sharks. Maybe it's a bullet or maybe---if you open your eyes---you will see that it's a flare.

Fasle Profit. I mean no offense to the devout. I admire your ability to believe in something bigger than yourself. Read this project. You might disagree with my ideals or perspectives, but you will not be able to deny the fact that I too believe in something bigger than me. This dying craft. It's slipping away to progress.

But what is progress? Before I write what I am about to write I'd like to say I am just as dependent on technology as the average indiviual of our times. Like I said before. I am a mirror. Not superior or inferior. Just saying it how I see it.

What is progress? This feels like it could be a fascinating long term project, but for the sake of this intro I'll just speak briefly on how I see it. As technology advances the patterns of history increase in pace. Like the sequencing of events happens with less space dividing them. As this process continues the cartilage that seperates the events erode. This is occuring for as far as I can tell because technology isn't the representation of the future. Rather it is the commodification and materialization of history. And make no mistake human history is a slaughter bench.

This craft. This craft of poetry and literature and artistry. It is not resistant to the future rather it is the reclaiming of destiny. It may be a faulty pursuit. In fact, I know that it is. The more we create in this way the more we enhance the capacity of developing technologies. But the point was never to win. The point was to fight. To fight the good fight, so to speak. I wear a Yankees cap, my blood might bleed orange, and it tastes like burbon, Fernet, and Guiness.

I chose to put "False Profit" on the cover of the paperback to shock and be disruptive. To realign people's perception of me. The months that have followed have been unique to say the least.

My life has been filled with extrordinary circumstances. The one that I am currently facing is potential homlessness as I squat in my current apartment. The controversy that followed the release of that previous project lead to a series of events that forced me to leave my job as an educator. I don't know how I am going to pay my bills. I don't know what will happen next for me. How unapologetically exciting.

This is what the journey looks like. My life couldn't be going worse, but I don't know where I am heading and that is how I know I am heading in the right direction.

This edition includes four new essays. *The Art of Loneliness, What is Freedom, Nowhere Man,* and *What is Hope. What is Hope,* feels like a more fitting foreward to this project, but for the sake of a certain asthetic it will remain in it's place with the other essays.

This updated edition will also include a ten part poem titled *Tomorrow Will Be Yesterday*. This is a poem that marked an extremely tumultous transition in my life. I read it at Bowery Poetry club in NYC. Something about the experience of reading this poem broke me in an extremely difficult and particular way. At the time I thought it broke me to nothing, but I now understand that it made me whole.

I am a very reserved person, but for the most part I am very approachable. Don't be afraid to let me know you hav engaged with my work. I don't blame you for taking part in my robbery. Whoever did it made fools of us all. The effect it had on the reader is more important to me then the money I lost. That doesn't mean I won't fight for what is mine, but don't let the guilt of that situation prevent you from approaching me with the love that I am learning to receive.

Please enjoy this book. I hope it does something for you. If it does nothing then my bad yo. Just know I tried my best. I, the individual, am for everyone, but I can understand if my art isn't.

One love. I am not a politicain. I prefer women to men. I have complicated trauama. Ketchup on your eggs is very acceptable. Mustard on hot dogs are not. Only poop when you are at home or at gas stations. Smell flowers when you can. Ask people if you can pet there dogs before you do. Buy your therapists gifts. Keep napkins in your glove compartment.

Metamorphosis

ruben d. encontrado

Contents

Dedication		iv
Dedication		v
Introduction to the Christmas Edition		vii
1	Introduction: Ghost Of A Good Poem	1
2	Drowning the Flame	5
3	Confessions of a Park Poet	7
4	Tomorrow Will Be Yesterday	105
5	Stone Upon Stone	131
6	Hope at Highest Point	169
Part Two		237
7	Nowhere Man	239
8	The Art of Loneliness	295
9	What is Hope?	309
10	What is Freedom?	315
About the Author		331

1

Introduction: Ghost Of A Good Poem

I have not received any compensation for my published writing. I own no NFT's. The only book of my writing I have published at the date of this publication is "Lame and Liminal: A collection of short stories". I have written a novel about hope. The working title was One More Cup Of Coffee. I eventually changed it to Tomorrow Will Be Yesterday. And a man's pursuit for it after the loss of the most romantic love he has ever known. THIS WORK IS INCOMPLETE AND UNPUBLISHED. As of right now. I have received no compensation for this writing and/or any of the paintings I have done under the alias "Ghost".

So, part one of this collection will be titled "A Drowning Flame". In the loneliest moment of my life I began to write poetry for the first time in over a decade. It was the only solace I could find as I separated myself from the world I had come to know. I was heartbroken and terribly lonely. "Confessions of A Park Poet" will capture the two years I spent immersed in nostalgia, busking, and fantastical love. How much of this window of my life is performative and how much of it was authentic, alludes me through the present truth and the immortalization of a romantic memory. The work I did feels so genuine and I am trying my best to not allow tarnished memories with others tarnish the memories of what I accomplished. For what I do know about this period in my life is that I was happy. Was I aligned with the truth at the moment in time, no, but I was happy. I deal with the truth now, that version of me gets to enjoy the bliss he felt.

The next section is what follows in my story. Utter collapse. And a slow debilitating rebuild. Learning how to write, again. Not write write, but reclaim my voice. How to think, again. How to be around others, again. Again. Again. Again. This section is called "Stone Upon Stone". Finally, the last segment of this collection are poems that come from a journal dedicated to new beginnings. Poems from the beginning of a new journey. As I leave the nest of my known reality and out into the world once more. A perpetual fuck up trying their best to be better. This section is titled, "Hope at Highest Point".

I am a Philosopher King. One of questions. Not one of answers. The only thing I do know is that I should probably quit. Lay my dreams to rest. Accept the tidal wave of our culture to wash me away. But I can't. I really wish I could stop being me and temporarily be someone I am not, but I just can't.

If I let go than what was the point of all that suffering? There has to be a point. For the ways I ceaselessly resisted the puniness that the hurt wanted me to be. For the ways that I continue to get back up and try again.

This is what I tell myself, but in reality when all one has is themselves, how can they ever be expected to let go?

How much more redemption must I go through before the hurt begins to make sense? Or is the point that it doesn't? That it was never meant to?

There was this lake I would go to by myself. One time while I was there a goose attacked me. It chased me down the pier. Then as I drew it away a young couple walked out on to the pier. Laughing at the way this bird was bullying me. At some point I got far enough away and the goose made it's way back toward the pier. Now the young laughing couple were cornered. I set up my lawn chair and watched with great enthusiasm as one went left and the other went right. Do geese quack? They make some noise, but is the term quaking reserved for ducks and doctors? Regardless of the fact they ran down the pier, laughing harder than they were before. I remember it was the first time I felt joy in months. Watching them lovingly evade the very thing they mocked.

    I'd go to that park often. I'd journal and read. Drink tea and gaze out on the still lake. I went there once with this girl I once knew. We sat in a tree and split an orange. We knew nothing, but enough back then. If I could go back to that moment knowing what I know now things would have been a lot different. My memories used to be filled with her eclectic outfits and contagious laughter. I'm glad that version of me got to enjoy them when he could.

    I wonder if there is anything in this world as pure as a playful imagination. I do not care to theorize other possibilities....

    I wish I knew why I feel so distant from the blood in my veins. I wish I knew why I have such violent memories and only hear stories of peace. I wish I knew why some songs make me cry and why other ones make me angry. I wish I could melt like butter on a pan. Be blown away like seeds of a dandelion. Or to slowly watch the pigmentation of my skin dilute until the moment where I was undeniably see through. Watch my stream of consciousness become a bubble. Float towards the sky and pop in the sun.

    And then for some reason, I think, nah, life is worth living. I'll go on. Almost instinctively. That hasn't always been the case, but it is now. All the while, life has never been more challenging for me. Habitually, I view life as a tragedy. And it has arguably never been more tragic. As a coping mechanism I am choosing to view things from a very ironic lens. I have to laugh at how stupid and moronic I have been and what I have been through. Or else I will not have the mental fortitude to do the one true obligation I have: KEEP PUSHING FORWARD. SIEMPRE ADELANTE.

My gratitude to the reader. Your support may seem like it goes unheard, but I assure you that it is not. My appreciation is expressed in my willingness to be vulnerable. I hope I make you feel something.

Enter.
Poetry.
Libertad.
<u>Soy.</u>
I was.
<u>I am.</u>
I will be.

2

Drowning the Flame

This is the poetry of a man who used to busk in Central Park under the name of Ruben De Escapado. He now goes under the name of ruben encontrado. It is a collection of about five years worth of poetry. Beginning from a time of solitude, then that of flattery and love, isolation and betrayal, and the pursuit of redemption. Throughout the course of these five years he frequently wrote until pens ran out of ink. This is a collection of one with little talent and ability, but of extreme resolve and dedication. Pursuing their dream with tunnel vision because others told him he could not achieve it.

ruben encontrado self-identifies as an activist and absolutely ridiculous. It is his hope that as you follow the trajectory of his writing you witness the shedding and becoming of the self that we go through in the pursuit of truth in this challenging life. You are deeply appreciative for your support.

3

Confessions of a Park Poet

Poems from May 2020 - October 2022

Making it up as I go.

But that's the sign. It reads, "All greatness is misunderstood.". Then I get on the train. None of us know each other, but we all know each other.

There is a Don Quixote statue on my desk. It has scotch tape holding the spear in his hand. I love it. He was too strong and whole before. Don Quixote is a broken man who refuses to give up.

Thank you to the countless who have supported me throughout collecting these poems and in the endeavors in which they were created.

None of you are forgotten.

Commentary on this section of poetry in retrospect:

I have my dog, my studies, my routine, and faith. I have faith in an ideal of goodness---from my understanding this is the foundations of all belief. I dug for the truth that I could feel but not see. As a result the integrity of my memories have lost much of their credence. But what cannot be taken from me is the perspective I ascertained amidst the lies. How I arrived at such wonderful outlook may have been grounded in dishonesty, but the heights of beauty and love I experienced are mine to keep. Whether the tree was plotted or grew from seed to mighty oak, it is I who climbed it's branches and witnessed such vast horizons.

These are poems from that time. When I would carry my smith and corona typewriter, her name is Celeste, and a sign that read "Pick a Topic, Get a Poem" to Central Park and busk almost every weekend for a year. There are buskers who have been doing it for longer. Poets of significantly greater talent. But I had entered a dream and I was pouring myself into my work to remain in that dream. A fairy-tale of love, activism, and peace.

These are the poems of Ruben De Escapado. He wrote until he died in Central Park. I am something different now. I have gone under many different names since. It's a strange thing to use a name that is not your own.

I live in a different state now. My name is no longer "Ruben the Escaped" but "Ruben the Found". My dog is sleeping by my feet. I am sipping on a chilled red wine. My apartment has a rocking chair on the patio. I am sitting on it as it sits in a valley. The sun is slowly slipping behind the mountain range. The clouds are large as they resist the urge to rain. The right profile is bathed in a soft peach. A peach a bit too ripe.

I re-read these poems in disbelief. I long for NY. I miss the subway rides and the scurrying streets. I miss the hikes and riverfront of my hometown, Ossining. I miss who I was to others before the truth had surfaced through the lies. But more than anything I miss my park bench. I miss hearing the countless covers of Frank Sinatra and the Beatles. I miss people watching. I miss existing in that cosmopolitan vortex, while knowing Harlem is twenty minutes one way, Brooklyn forty five the other, and my favorite museum lets me in with a library card. It is only fifteen minutes away. I miss feeding squirrels. I miss getting into debates about the fundamental issues of reality with strangers from Spain, Morroco, and Japan. I miss talking about the existence of God in a time lacking peace with priests and those fascinated by prophets. I miss talking to hippies from California about the big bang and the creation of all things. I miss talking to Guatemalans about what happens after death. I miss talking to mothers from Kansas about sunsets from beyond a field. I miss talking to farmers from Maine about their bison ("People think because of the way they look that they are aggressive, but they are really quite gentle. When you spend time with them they become quite affectionate. Very intelligent animals. I use them to remove fallen trees from the surrounding woods….I am going to find a nice tree to sit under and read your poem."), Emily Dickinson, St.Micheal flowers, and that time of day where sun is gone but the light remains in silence. I miss listening to the homeless about their struggle. I miss having psychiatrists asking if I'd be willing to listen. I miss off duty police officers showing me their poetry. I miss the look in a stranger's eyes as they read my poem. But more than anything, I miss being a version of myself that believed they deserved a version of love solely conjured up for fairy tales.

I don't know what tomorrow will bring---I barely have a grasp on the past, but I am optimistic. I think things might be alright. If they're not, then I take solace in knowing I tried.

Back to the poetry.

NOISE
There isn't much

Holding it all together.
Decaying...
Slowly eroding away.
It is a real rat bastard that way,
Nibbling away at our trust.
Kindness.
Compassion.
Thinned out
And discredited.
Nobody believes nobody.
Everybody has got it worse.
When all of that is gone,
What else will time take?
Will it try to take me?
Will it try to take you?
I like to think, no.
No, it can't.
These eyes
These ears
This mouth
This voice
These are mine
These are yours.
There are too many instruments
In this orchestra of ontology
How can we deny ourselves?
When we are the experience
Of this mad city?
There are sirens
Ambulance or police
It makes no difference
They won't get there in time.
Or maybe they will

That's the part I never remember
The other side of the lie
Subway doors open
The carts scream around each bend.
Cabs speed
Cars honk.
They need to get where they are going,
Suppose, We all do.
Sounds burst and blare.
Setting this city—
This wonderfully mad
Drunk on life city—
Setting it all to flames.
Flames that are thorough
Flames that are true
That not even the rats of time can escape.
I see the homeless ooze with ecstasy.
I see the wealthy crushed by the weight of their shadow.
I see tourists
To them, it's all a magical mystery.
Midnight; twilight; crystal light.
Those above the sut and stench
They are deaf to it all.
They can't see the eclectic zoo
Colors and noises.
Sounds and views.
Reserved for the mad
For the lonely
For those gripped by the spirit of the road
Reserved for me
Reserved for you.
Breathing in subway steam
Breathing in conversations

Muffled and blended.
Who did this
Who didn't do that
Will the project be done on time
I'll have the rent by Monday
Noise. Noise. Noise.
Loud intrusive.
Loud and intrusive noise.
Space. Type. Space.
Prose.
Stanza.
A poem.
Silence.
Silently sitting
My typewriter with me.
Serenity; be still.
I find peace.
I find it in this oasis of a park.
I find it somewhere
Echoing within.

MY SOUL IS A LONELY HIGHWAY
We all know the lonely hallway.
Maybe it's the shadow over the door.
The tired paint.
A break in aesthetics.
Unlocking the door.
Unlocking the mind.
The child gazes,
So vertigo may live
Just below my ribs.
Despite the trampoline of my guts

I gaze
The child gazes
Longing to explore this unknown.
Beyond the door.

Shivering with fear.
Explore at your own risk.
We cannot guarantee
Safety.
Things can't be the same
The way they were before.

One day I twisted the nob,

I nap on tables
Swim in murky water
Stardust serpents reflect in starlight.
Shaky hands of Night paint the moon on river.

I am on the road.
Writing to you from beyond the hallway.
Yes—it is scary.
Yes—it is daunting.
Yes...
Each stride pulls you further.
Further from who you were.
But beyond the hallway,
The carpets are replaced by blacktop.
Tired paint becomes pastures
Becomes mountains.

Twist the knob.
Twist the ignition.

There are clay canyons to be slept in.
Oceans opposite
To be walked through
Swam through
Floated upon

A west rifle way displays
On the left
A sea of mountain green
On the right
A sea of red refraction
Nirvana has No Name, Colorado.
These waves reach over me
As I burrow further
And further
Into my hallway
Crescents collide
Burying me in the sea of rubble
Returning me to soil
Soil from which I was birthed.

To be born again.

So, I write to you from beyond the door
The door of many forms
Beyond the lonely hallway
Beyond the friend, you didn't get to hug
Beyond the person, you wished you loved
I write to you
To say
Twist the knob
Twist it
Twist and don't look back.

Until river reflections
Show you that looking back
Is the hallway's current flow
The human condition
Big sign
White and gold
On that viva Las Vegas strip

Until we accept the hallway
We can never see the Highway
Comma
Man.

ALONE AT SEA
Two years ago,
I wrote daily drafts
Of my own demise.
A writer who can never
Get the words right.
Tongue-tied when saying goodbye
Needle knives resting under my spine.
Pricking my being.
Stabbing my will.
Will to power.
Will to live.
To die.
To cry.
To lie.
Lying in the face of reflections.
Reflections. Reflections. Reflections.
Retracted-Refracted-Fractured
Introspection.

Showed me the colors—
Or how they've dimmed,
Under the thousands of scabs, I have picked.
Leaving me hard and dry
Where beautiful skin
Once felt the love...
Of family kisses
Of warm bed sheets
The Night of Christmas.
I wrote and wrote and wrote and wrote
Chasing words that left my heart
Numbing my fingers and toes
Numbing everything I thought I had known
Leaving me writing empty words.
I reach---
Just shy of the wordless feelings I am after
They always lacked weight
No! it felt worse than that.
I sank deeper than that.
This surface level
Let them drown the way you drowned.
That way, they can learn too.
It was worse than worse but also pleasantly bliss
To not care.
Lose my mind a bit.
Stare down the deep end of the cliff.
Just to get pulled off the edge.
But now I have the words within my grasp
The words come to me so naturally
I can barely stop
Leaving me writing about
Grassy fields
And winds of leaves

And pale blue skies
That only
Only on my good days, I can see.
Or at least that's what I told myself.
That the sky only showed when
I have meditated.
Slept well.
And returned to myself.
Returned home.
Back to the thoughts of deep knives
In the depths of my belly.
Spewing out words into the world
Green grass stained red
Got me out of fucking bed.
My imminent demise
Somehow stopped my tears.
Upon my dry cheek,
Words began to flow
My heart was clear like snow.
Clear like snow?
See what I mean!
The words just come and go
And go
And go and go
Going and gone.
Home runs in central park!
Without knowing, they return.
My head is a dry pen. No ink?
Just give it a shake
Suddenly there are words, again.
So, I write and write and write
Hoping for bad days again.
Knowing that good ones are

Just around the bend.
So, I dive head first
Not knowing how shallow
This pool of infinity
Extends.
Slamming keys and pressing send
Looking back on my broken introspection
Seeing where the words went wrong
I felt them in a moment
I felt them in a song.
I am going nowhere again...
And that is okay.
Because when I go
My passion for the words will always stay
So when I imagine the noose
Around my neck
Snapping! me
Pulling me to my next show
Every time I think of anything embarrassing, really.
First dates
Fifth-grade birthdays
Saying I love
A soul of hate
Saying I miss you
Life is great
If things go wrong, then write.
I can always rely on my neck tightening, again.
And again. And again.
Life infinitely trudging on.
My mind is sharp like a saw
A saw that blows my shoulder out
As I wonder how it went wrong
How it went wrong always feels

So obvious to the miserable man
Of nowhere land.
But what went right is what the good days
Try to show me.
Pale-blue me.
Reaching above the world.
Reaching above me
Reaching beyond my reach to see
What I can touch and see.
What I can teach and feel.
Sitting in seiza amongst my misery.
Sitting in seiza amongst my absurdity.
Sitting in seiza with
Broken memory.
Of shards of glass--
Of shards of past that
Cut my hands---
Cut my mind.
Giving me bloody ink.
Gives me plenty of material to work with.
So I slam the keys and repeat again,
Wonder when the hangman will knock again.
I slam my keys and call it prose
Prophetically writing proper praise
Prophetically philanthropize
Apparently presenting
Presence as a present
Preserved and profound
Providing professionals
Proclamations of…
Endless times
Rises and sets
Where I find my will to live.

Just to misplace my happiness
As soon as I pick up my pen.
Again. Again. Again.……..

CONFESSIONS OF A PARK POET
"What's your name?"
A question I have been
Actively trying to ask more.
At least as of recent.
People come up to me.
They ask for poems
Expecting fortune-telling.
Wisdom. Prophecy. Remedy.
Or worse.
They want to know about me.
How did I start doing this?
They ask.
How do we do anything?
I ask.
Joke.
Deflect.
My chest screams:
My face smiles.
A "V" for victory on my hand.
They wonder what my experiences must be like
Sitting out here on a park bench?
Talking to strangers?
Doing what I love?
Their pupils tremble under the pressure
of their fleeting patience.
The little they are holding on to
Is digging deep into their palms
So, I tell them the good

About the poems
Of wedding bands
Of loving couples
Of those still holding on
They smile.
Can you do that for me?
Here are my broken pieces
Do they fit your eyes?.
Let me know what you can see
Put them in your eyes.
Can I get a selfie?
I smile with tears that bleed.
I am a little bit broken.
You're a little bit sad.
Holding you together.
While holding up me.
A history with painful pleasures.
I continue to slaw away.
Burying all of it deep within
Under my typewriter
Below my seat
Deep-deep below the roots
Of pavement flowers
To be eaten by worms of past.
The blackest ink of me.
I omit to those catching their breath
Poems of
Postpartum mothers
Flushed cheeks
Streaming tears.
New fathers throwing their wallets.
All reason is out the window.
She believed what he had been saying

All because I happen to say it too.
The baby will be okay.
They will be too.
No knowing.
Only trying.
I omit that story.
I omit,
Girls crying over boys.
Boys trying to win the girl back.
I omit the gay man
Who's years of longing for more
Longing to be heard
Longing to be looked at
Is fulfilled by my mere willingness
To see his heart and be one too.
Turning me into an object
Of fantasy
One that quenches a desperate thirst
A thirst for decency.
Leaving me on a cold bench
More a statue of an idea.
Less a lonely poet with a dream.
Less a person.
To all the story seekers
I omit the countless
Lesbians
Transgenders
Blacks
Asians
Latinos
Middle-easterners.
Arabs
Whites

Catholic
Jews
Muslims
Buddhists
Outcasts
Misfits
Loners
Freaks
Broken like glass, people.
Who are desperate for magic
Magic from a stranger
Who are baffled
Someone will listen
Because someone
Sees the person
Before the classification of their satisfaction
Who they are within
A willingness to love
A willingness to believe
A demand for a better country
How they get through their day
What they see in the mirror
In a world of don't
Tread on me
In a world of don't
Offend me
We label
And label
Boxing people into categories
Designed for ideas
Not individuals.
Leaving no room for compassion.
Just rigid acceptance of circumstance

Some things are so out of our control
They feel normal
Did I just say that?
No matter what
We are people
Human beings
Dealing with human shit
So when people come to me
A man desperate to survive
In a world
Where he relates more to a dog on a chain
Where the breeze he is trying to be
Is better weighed down.
Weighed down by the jeopardy of my being
When they come to me, looking
For spiritual salvation
I omit the girl
Far too young
Asking me for a poem about loneliness
A girl with beautiful blue eyes
A girl with a decoration of scars on her wrist
An abstract mutilation
An outward expression
Of the internalization
Of a young spirit
Compartmentalized into a world
Where nobody quite understands
Despite sharing the same pains
I omit
That I think of her everyday
I omit
that I regret not exchanging more information
that I am haunted by the fact

that I don't know if she is okay
if what I said
if what I wrote
was enough
that I can't fucking believe
I didn't ask for her name.
I omit and omit.
Not because I want to lie.
I omit
Because these feel like my burdens
I see it in all your eyes
You can barely handle yourselves
I'll keep taking the weight
For now
My shoulders are broad
For now
But the days I am not there
The exhibit moves from the bench
I am picking up my pieces
Becoming whole again.
But when I am out there…
I have been doing a better job of asking,
"What is your name?"

TRAIN RIDES
A man enters stage right
Of the subway car.
He stands; I sit.
He nods; I nod.
Where does his hairline end?
His eyebrows start?
Nonetheless.
Handsome or hideous.

He contributes to mine.
I contribute to his.
A canvas of loneliness
Painted by the scenery of
Unfamiliar familiar faces.
Eggshell eyes glossed over
With internal conflict.
Faces wishing to be elsewhere
But they are here.
You are here.
We are here.
So, We ride---
Within and without our desires.
A man nods.
A wordless conversation
Of empathy.
Sorrow sews us spiritually.

She sits; I admire.
A nervous smile; I nod.
New Yorkers have resolute necks.
Man and woman across a lonely aisle.
We contribute to fantasies.
Fantasies that keep the hopeless warm at Night.
MINE: I tuck her hair behind her ear
She fantasizes the same?
She blushes; I was right.
She was beautiful
Scarlet hair hides freckled cheeks.
But I couldn't save her
Too busy saving myself.
Far too busy.
So, I exit stage left.

Stepping on the platform.
Killing our hopes
And a cockroach.
That my shoe spreads down fifth avenue.

FORGOTTEN POEM
This poem is not coming to me.
It was a fantastic idea.
Life-changing,
Timeline-altering idea.

I thought of it while
Running by a still lake.
It was something about loneliness.
How still water makes it bearable.
There is still water in love.
And loneliness when running.
Not always physical.
But running towards.
Or running from.

It was a good poem.
That I am sure of.
If only I could remember.

I thought of it while
Staring at a mountain.
It was something about…
Patience
Pressure.
How mountains are patient under infinity.
And the pressure of infinitely not existing.
Not always not existing.

But not not existing.
Or not existing.

It was a good poem.
That I am sure of.
If only I could remember.

I thought of it while
Walking through a cemetery.
It was something about a singular truth.
Could it exist?
How there is peace in death.
That chaos is a human invention.
Not always the only truth.
But running towards.
Or running from.
Not always the only truth.
But not not existing.
Or not existing.

It was a good poem.
That I am sure of.
If only I could remember.

It's horribly beautiful

There is a child within me.
Poor bastard is scared.
He watches what time does.
To other people.
To me.
I look in the mirror.
The only familiar part

Are these eyes staring back.
Those are the child's eyes.
Gently squinting in the sun.

He is a speck
In the bleakness of being.
But from time to time:
A woman will smile,
A toddler will laugh,
A moon will hang in a day-lit sky.
The child fills his eyes.
Sending tears into my skull.
These tears.
These purple electrical tears.
Run down spine.
Make their way to my fingers and toes.

Encumbering me.
I embrace it.
All of it.
This horribly alluring ambiguity of being.
It is mine.
Mine to own.
I hold it.
The child too.
He is safe.
He believes me.
But it is too much life to bear.
Retreating within.
Leaving an essence
That slips through my fingers.

Yet something lingers,

Existing in Plato's heaven
Next to the number two and wooden pipes.
The memory of him.
Or the memory of me.
Like most things, I can't decide.
So, I put on Miles Davis
And imagine pink trees blooming in the spring.

Sometimes, it is a pleasure

I very frequently feel—
Nothing.
Then everything all at once.
Randomly.
A child's smile in a setting sun.'
A beautiful ear held by a jealous wind.
I see the mountain;
Therefore, I am the mountain.
Then nothing, again.

Before I could accept
'Nothing' was as natural as
Fucking
Breathing
And fucking.
I used to think this made me depressed.
Sick. Yuck. Life in a rut.
But thinking I was depressed
Made me more fucking depressed
Then the depression I was feeling.
Unbeknownst I doubled down.

A person looked over the valley.

There was red rock and a deep river.
They thought, as an eagle cawed in the distance,
"Warry when walking in the water,
West water wanders
Step within; be washed away."
Don't be upset when the current takes ya
Was the conclusion of the day.

But realistically,
You have a high capacity for emotion.
And.
If this world is overwhelmingly miserable.
And.
We know everything exists only in its opposite.
Then.
It must be overwhelmingly beautiful.
Meaningful and alive.
Silent and silent.
We receive substance.
Then create the subject.

In this dancing battle.
Of Night and Day
Life astray.
Mysterious magic
Of the imagination
Be a gentleman.
Never let her dance alone.
You can bear any pain
To savor the view.

A poem in February

Fewer conversations.
More expectations.
You wonder why
I sit and listen,
Never a word to share.
Acting like I have no cares?
Yet I expand—
More
And
More...
Aware?
That's *why* does or doesn't.
Sit or dance.
Watch or act.
Cry or hold the hand.
Listen and listen.
To all your expectations,
But if we had a conversation.
A real conversation.
Would the weight off my shoulder?
Make your hands blister?

Trippin with strangers
The world loves clothes.
Light and satin—
But naked dawns
Leave me alone.
Singular in the binary coding
Of my feeble introspection.
Next to cigarette burns
Wet dreams
Pulsing cock
Wincing eyes

Twisting-turning toes
Of a society with no clothes.
Army helicopters
Thuga-thuga-thuga by.
I am an ant,
Minute and miniature.
But it is an accessory to my day—
The sky is always blue.
Even when it looks grey.
The sky is always blue.
Except for the naked dawn.
Of trembling toddlers
Dressed in suits and ties,
Vote left.
Vote right.
Upside down—
Inside out—
Give me a jive
Keep me alive
Our votes don't matter
At night time
Our votes don't count on the six-line.
Where some fungi festers
Spawning spiritual salvation of
Artists, Souls, Desperation.
Reeking of
Artists, Rats, and pollution.
Buddhist's huddle.
Mothers cloak children
One percent doesn't matter down here.
A man screams with a voice from hell.
Drumming the drum in Satan's chest.
Buddhist's huddle.

Mothers cloak crying children.
There is a woman
Tired and beautiful,
She sings Aretha Franklin.

You've slipped again
I haven't written like this to you
In quite a while.
I still have the address.
The cave in my chest,
Is where you reside.
I hold on tighter
As you push me away.
Leaving us violently dancing
A song of now--
A song of once was--
A song of what is to come.
Some days I hold you;
So tight.
Never loosening my grip.
Smothering you as you push me away.
A song of now—
A song of once was—
A song of what is to come.
Then I hold you there
Suspended in the abyss.
A trapezius with flexed triceps.
Gripping you just above
The nighttime laughter.
Just for my grip to be too tight.
Just for you to push too far.
Holding on desperately
To each other

In different directions
This free fall.
Hand in hand.
For your smiles are brighter,
When my eyes are looking.
For your voice is sweeter,
When I am listening.
For your lips,
They feel different...
As they release mine.
I look at you and—

First day back; many away
I am out here again.
I am breathing slowly.
I am out here again.
"The spoken word."
"Spreading joy."

To all that know me—
The world is yours,
For all your holding.
So, run at life
Like nothing is holding.
Just know they hold me.
Because life is good.
Good at holding.

Untitled
There are days.
Often days
As regular as

Monday
Wednesday
Overpriced lattes.

There are days
Often days where
I don't wear hoodies
But I put my hood up.

There are days.
Often—
Frequent days where
"Don't let me down."
Is on a loop
More circular than a Beatle.
I have never known.

On these days
I walk slowly.

Sunshine days.

Rainy day gloom.

I did what we were supposed to do.

But the doom looms.
I face the sun
Like Whitman told me too.
But the shadows
Are still all around me.

There are days

Often days—
Frequent days—
Painfully frequent days.
Where I wonder,
What if they stopped?
Debt
Loneliness
Struggle
Suffering
Scars under the skin
That nobody can see
But I can't help but feel
What if it all stopped?
Who would care?

Someone dusts their bookshelf
They bought a new duster
They wipe the books clean.
A great display for
When the guests come over.
A man
Abandoned his family.
At least that's how
His kids will see it
As they enjoy the
Roof. Blankets. Food.
While he calicles his hands
In foreign lands
Where he refuses to learn the language.
Right now, the hate
Is just noise
Vibrating his ignorant ears.

I know,
I know.
My situation isn't bad.
I walk by people
As they smack their gum
With their sunglasses on.
My tee-shirt shows me
Scars that only I can know.
I put my hood up.
Retreat into myself.
Thinking about how easy
I have got it.

Rust Bucket
The third book in a trilogy.
Over a bowl of ramen.
Studying the soup.
Devouring the book.

Silent. Alone.
Not lonely.
Or maybe—
Not sure,
The book and chopsticks
Occupy my mind.

The soup gets old.
I grow cold.
Same with the story.
So, I leave this Dolphin Hotel.
To roam different waters.

A fishbowl of a car

Stopped at the crosswalk.
I look, really taking her in.
I imagine her skin?
It resembles her grey Toyota.
Old. Rusty. Worn. Flakey.
Like cracking leather.
Cold and old.

My poem.
My book.
My story.
My soup.
This lady.
With her coffee-stained
Teeth.
Car.

Cosmopolitan
Spick here.
Gringo there.
That's at least what I tell myself

Emotional Anorexic
It is sunny.
Warm.
Possibly beautiful.
Birds are chirping.
Butterflies in the wind.
Instinctually…
I grab my umbrella.

Expurgate
A machine clunks forward.

Each piece being held together
By another, that was placed to hold up the first.
And so on, and what not, and so it goes.
Take it with a grain of salt.
What are you gonna do?
That's life, ya know.
And shut the hell up!
A Jenga-locomotive propelled forward.
Forwards all we know.
That one tap, touch, pull, quiver,
Or quake of truth will send
Normalized-culturized-family-ties-internalized
(Silence is a lie)
Crash and burn!
Burn and crash!
Illuminated faces at midnight!
Drink whiskey by the flames!!!

Bipolars called crazy,
Here comes the hurricane.
Depressives called quiet,
The calm before the storm.
Anxiety called nervous,
Get out of its way.
CRASHING!
CRASHING!
CRASHING!
Crash like lightening striking glass.
Generational trauma burns
As it slams into the two-way mirror
Of confused, misconstrued pasts.

On one side, an appending reflection

Of our machine as it consumes.
The last honest men.
The last benevolent women.
On the other side, swimming pools
Of empty truth, but we are empty,
False and ugly.

At least we can pretend.
You sons of fucks!
I wish I were loyal to you,
And not the truth!
I wish I loved you
And not the truth.
Oh, how I wish!
Oh, the tragedy of Quixote!
Someone get Sancho out of my ear!
If only...
If only we could ask the dead
About LOYALTY.
If only we could ask infants
About LOVE

The long road
Can't see shit.
He told me to walk.
30 days in the sun.
A delinquent desperado
Ties his laces.

30 days later.
Him and his skin.
Tired and tan.
He tells the man,

"All I can see
Is that you are
A fool.".

From a former abyss
Fear the gaze of the abyss.
Fear more the absence of the gaze.

Better to face the heart of darkness,
Then let it consume you in the Night.

Better to be a man who has witnessed,
Then to be an abyss of a man.
Filled with loathsome ignorance
Where wonder should be.

Trust Issues
Scar tissues.
Fogs. Blurs. Obscures.
The line between
Trust and happiness.

Shit (life)(existence)(love)
Is fucking cruel.
Feels like it takes
More than it gives.
Only sometimes.

We forget.
Pain hurts more than
Happiness feels good.
So, we are generous with our love.
People can only take pieces.

Hopeless romantics
Turned casual lovers.
Pretending not to care
Because we care too much.

Hoping someone will save us.
We are drowning in the pool
We jumped in.
Asking for help
Without helping ourselves.

The only way to trust again,
Is to trust again.

Nowhere man
I am a writer;
Also
I am nobody;
Also
I am everyone.

(Depends on the insecurity available)

I write for nobody.
I write for me.
I like nobody.
He is a good man.
I write for nobody.

Against the current

Grab her hand.
Pull her in.
Hold her tight-- sorrow sinks.
Let it sink.
Deep into your chest.
Into a sea of your strength.
You've weathered the storm.
So, we hold on tight.

She is warmth in winter.
Lemonade in summer.
Comfort you forgot you had.
Don't speak.
No need.
She needs to be held.

So, we hold on tight.
Tighter than ever before.
Against the current.
Older than we were.
Younger than we will be.
A time. A place. A moment.
Forever and forgotten.

So, we hold on tight.
Not to be loved.
Always to love.
For what else is there?

When did I get a cat?
"There are three versions of me.
One who ordered pizza (love that guy)
One impatiently waiting (right now)

One eating that cheesy goodness (lucky bastard)
The three me-s move forward together.
Soon it will be eating that cheesy goodness.
Wishing I had a lactose pill.
Never wanting pizza again.
One dies off.
Another is born.
What is my gain?
My net profit?
Am I in three places at once?
Death, life, birth.
To exist is to die in reverse?
Am I spread too thin?
That would explain why.
Why I don't feel like myself.
Which one is the true me?
The obvious answer is the now.
But all versions have and will think.
To think is to be.
Even now, I am thinking
About how I thought
I was going to think now
And my thoughts now will be
What I was thinking then.
If I manipulate my thoughts later
So that 'now' is correct
Aren't I living in the past?
Or is that the future?
Do they negate making me present?
Do you see my predicament?"

He licks his paw, stands up, and leaps—
Off the couch with grace.

Right before exiting the room, he looks back
Over his shoulder and says,
"Listen, man. I am just a fucking cat.
I got my own shit I am dealing with."
The phone rang.
My Chinese food was here.

Move

Waves crash.
Lightning strikes,
Thunder roars,
Birds soar,
And we—
We bleed.
There is a road west.
Calling our spirits.
So, I am heading there.
As my soul shifts from
Saxophone to harmonica.
I see my crown of thorns
Still makes me bleed.
But I am in a swarm of warriors
Barreling forward on 66.
We are Highwaymen.
Midnight riders.
Shotgun-wielding Dharma Bums:
Quixote.
Sgt. Pepper.
Mad Ahab.
Sisyphus.
The fool himself.

Moving. Bleeding.
Taking the blood from our eyes.
Licking our lips.
Moving and bleeding.
Bleeding and moving.
Gallons. Rivers. Seas.
Vast oceans of our blood.
The leviathan of our being
Needs somewhere to swim.
Move and bleed.
Bleed and move.
Seeing. Touching. Smelling. Hearing.
Living!
This country.
As it slips through the fingers of opinion.
Never to be gripped again.
Like the waves that crash against our past.
So,
We roar like thunder.
Drive like lightning.
Soar like birds.
Bleed.
Move.
As if we will never
Do it again.

Bukowski (sometimes)
Timepieces,
Out of time.
Feel like Bukowski—
Maybe more like Hank.

If only I had a cat,
Cheap whiskey,
Cheap women,
Cheap cigarettes.

But that damn will live.
It is at it again.

The only cheap thing
Are my socks,
Are my attitude,
Are my shoes,
My cigarettes.
Don't have tobacco.
They don't make me feel like Hank
More like Lao Tzu.
I am only Bukowski,
Sometimes.
Ironically enough
Only when I got money to spend.

To doubt is to be
Birth (physically).
Taught. Misguided.
Meaning in the meaningless.
Pain. Doubt. Learn.

Time costs innocence.
See with new eyes.
Tears break them in.
Meaningless in the meaningless.
Pain. Doubt. Learn.

Death (not physically).
Know it's your fault.
Meaningless in meaning.
Pain. Doubt. Learn.

Birth (not physically).
Time returns innocence.
Walk an inch above the ground.
Meaning in meaning.
Live. Grow. Love.

Death (Physically).
Move on.
Nutrients in soil.
Rest. Relief. Reborn.
As a tangerine.

Idiot dog
The fucker barked at walls.
Nipped at ankles.
Shit on the carpet.
Ate the wires.

Wobbled with a hanging tongue
On her way to find fleas.
I couldn't get mad.
She didn't know.
Good or bad,
That's a human curse.

All there was
Is what we create—

What we don't.
All was forgiven
When she slept under my arm.

Diverged in a yellow wood
The canvas of our existence
Will lack color.

Tongues sorrowfully singing,
"What could have been?"

Confined. Jailed. A captive.
To the opinion of others.

Hollowed out by the lies
we dig deep within.

Blaming circumstances when
Reflections hold the truth.

Turn left at the light

MY EYES.
How the fuckers have changed.
They saw things differently back then.

When I made ripples in tides
Of oceans
Of lilies
And currents of wind.
North was south—
Or maybe west
Never mind. Never mind.

I remember it was east of Eden.
Southwest?

After soccer.
After school.
After karate.
After play dates.
Birthday parties.
Boy scouts.
When in doubt?
Turn left at the light by the oak tree.
Left at the light.
And you were home.

From Ice cream cones.
Home alone. Virginity thrown.
Left at the light.
Always meant HOME.

Went away for a while.
Desolation within my depression.
Real atonement of the soul.
Section 8 was
My monastery of poverty.

Been through too much.
Them too.
Wasn't scared about that.
Was afraid the left turn was different.
That when I pulled into the lane.
It was just another lane.
A turning lane of New York.
America.

Earth.

Put it off for months.
Years maybe, it's all a blur.
I won't tell.
Ashamed of my fear.
Eventually, there was no choice.

Turned left with my life in a truck.
Hugged my family.
Some friends too.
Good to have you back, they said.
Good to be back, I'd say.
Somewhere between my tears
Of gratitude and regret.
I Unpacked—
got back in my car.
Went down to the river.
It had been too long
Since I had last skipped rocks.

Random thoughts on rainy afternoons

Summer daze
Hand raised
Fifth grade
Childhood glaze

I am not with them
But am with others.
I am not with others
But am with them.
All the above?

None of the above.

Melting pots of liquid gold.
My thoughts:
Behold what I've been told
Since four years old.
Bad is new.
Good is old.
Scold and fold.
Conform and mold.
Inside myself,
Restrain and hold.
I am young,
My soul is old.
I am hot,
The world is cold.
I am cold,
The world is colder.
I am colder,
The world is the coldest.
What's colder then coldest?
I don't know—
My brain bubbles.
Too much in its melting pot of
Smells and smog and secrets and serendipity
And silence.
Silence.
Silent is the sea to the sleeping serpent.
Silent is the song to the poisoned pastor.

Summer daze.
Hand raised.
Fifth grade.

Childhood glaze.
Heart a blaze.

Melting pots of liquid gold.
Reek of lacquer and rubber.
Silent is the sleeping pastor
Poisoned and punished
To the serendipitous sea.

At my typewriter #1 (CP)
Sometimes I miss heartbreak
I hate that it's the case
    Like an old war veteran
    Thinking a good war
    Is all this economy needs
    The jobs it will produce
    This is the burden
    This is the poison
    The poet-philosopher
    We crave pain
    Long for it even
    It's honest
    It's real
    But somewhere between
    My self-sabotage
    And my paranoia
    I find myself selfishly
    Craving the love I reject
    Thinking somehow
    Or someway
    It will repair the damage
    I inflict
    Because I am hurt

And will hurt you too

At my typewriter #2 (CP)
Ain't no denying
I love this shit
Obsessed to the point
Of putting myself
In harm's way
My toes are cold
My nose is shot
This shadow over the sun
Is the devil coming
Trying to take me to the warm underbelly
Certifying my corpse
Is good and cold
On the days like today
I die.
The mad poet indeed loses it
But these are the days that
Need to happen
It is the only way to remember
How beautiful it is to live
But god fucking damn
I am cold
Cold as I can be
Don't think about it
What an expensive price to pay
I always thought you paid with cash
Looks like I am going to pay with my toes

At my typewriter #3 (CP)
I am here again
As I will be

Moving forward
I am here again
And this time
A homeless woman
Walks by me
Filthy—covered in rags
I smell her from beyond my mask
Another woman walks by
In a clean white coat
New shoes
The latest release
I am here again
Relating more to the woman
Who does not hide under what she has
But is much more
Because she has less.

At my typewriter #4 (CP)
Sirens wail in from the city
The city beyond the trees.
Someone is in need.
That's what they tell me.
Yet
But
Nonetheless
Nobody can know these lonely days
Not the way I do
A bit selfish that way
I know
But it can't be helped
I'm limited to my hurt
My hurt limited to me
That's what I like to think

Dylan only moves me
Just me
But then it plays in the park
A strangers phone
While the wind moves the leaves
Across the still ground
In which I am immovable
Like the stones that I rest upon
People walk by
Women smile
Some men too
As I sit a statue of something
In their imagination
As they walk by
And walk by
And walk by
And I am still as these stones
Listening to sirens wail in
From the city beyond the trees
That people are in
But I swear only I can see

Fear; overcoming it
Shaky knees
Trembling tendons
I feel weak
Where I have been told
My strength is.
I have failed
Just to fail again
And again and again.
If they are not the same,

Who remembers more
My body or me?
My mind or me?
Me or me or me.
But I wasn't then
So I won't be now.
I won't be now
So I am never there again.
Down nine times
Back up ten.
Journey of thousands of miles
The only way to win
Is to begin.

At my typewriter #5 (CP)
There are models in the park
They sit and pose
Looking beautiful in the cold
Suffering for a like
Suffering for a post
I try to relate
Or understand might be the better term
But all your looks
And your proclamations of beauty
Leave you in sinking sand
Despite all the lenses
You view yourself
Where the critique
Is never kind
You long for the approval of
People you cannot stand
They tell you what you want to hear
But you don't want them to say it

It isn't the voice
The voice of your own creation
The satisfaction can only come
From the inside
But what do I know
I am just a lonely poet
Sitting on a park bench
Listening to the
Saxophone
Violin
Accordion
Down the way
As you continue to pose
And I collect tips
Wondering why I should judge.

At my typewriter #6 (CP)
There is a bird crying
I hear it
It is just crying
Hopelessly crying
The desperation in its cries
I can't tell if it calls for
Help
Or mercy
Sitting here
Stuck on this park bench
In the cold, just like it
Watching as people pass me by
I clack on my typewriter
Bleeding as I type
I can't say with certainty
That there is a difference

Help
Or mercy
Can feel like one and the same
From the crying bird
Above the trees
With no name

Daydreaming of Her
I woke up to
A beautiful rising sun
Bathing the walls of our room
Loving kisses
A sleepless dream
Of you and me

Elsewhere and onward
Wherever I go
I was with you
"I believe in you."
Were the words
Your mouth produced.
"then I believe in me too."
Is what my brain injected
My mouth ejected

Elsewhere and onward
Wherever I go
There are pink clouds
A sunset view
Resting on top
Blooming tree branches
Foreground of tents
Gentle and blue

Elsewhere and onward
Wherever I go
Somehow
Always
Daydreaming of you.

Sometimes...
The south of France
A cottage overlooking a cloudy pasture.
Puerto Rico
In a colorful home of Viejo San Juan
Crash boat on the weekends.
Colorado.
Where we bathe together in a lake.
Mountaineering and navigating.
Rocky Mountain highs.
Somewhere in Spain,
Quenching our thirst
With a sweaty sangria.
Seoul, South Korea
In complete ambiguity
Smiling at our secret existence
Always a pasture
Pink leaves blooming
On gentle trees.

Holding you.

Most days...
Waking up
A beautiful rising sun
Bathing the walls of our room

Loving kisses
A sleepless dream
Of you and me.

At my typewriter #7 (CP)
There was a man and a woman
Standing on the train
Each one
A hand on the pole
A hand holding each other
Wordless—never silent
Passing by in the underbelly
Of New York
A woman sat next to me
She was reading something
Something I immediately assumed
Was not as good as my novel
Just assuming out of arrogance
Or confidence
Or competence
I can't really tell the difference
At least not anymore

Beautiful people convinced they are ugly
Let me show you
The way I see you
Even for an instant
The instant that fleets by
Just out of reach
Before I can even think
To hold it

To cherish it
To care for it
It is gone as quick as it happens.
A passing smile
Within a glimmering ribbon
Of purple
Of you.

At my typewriter #8 (CP)
Fuck, it is cold
I mean, really cold
Freeze your ass off
While daydreaming of
Islands with palm trees--cold.
But here I am
Infinitely in a state of 'again'
Hoping these strangers
Will put some money in my hands
I have bills
I have rent
Groceries
And my appetite to feed
I have written a book
A profound and powerful piece
I wanna save money
I wanna get it out too
But I starve and type
But I stave and wait
Hoping that tomorrow's freezing day
Will be my desperately needed break.

Moab

It's a long and distant river
That took me and my name
The sun fried my past
The water cooled my flame
And I rose from the red clay.
Knowing but one thing.
The tides are turning again.
The tides are turning.

At my typewriter #9 (CP)
It was noon
On a day on which
I remember nothing else
Other than the cup of coffee
The one I spilled
Or the mother and the daughter
They held each other as they wept
Or the single train cart
Going somewhere in reverse
It was sad and wonderful
All at once
Life
So it goes
What are you gonna do
Now it goes
Then it is gone.

Melancholic melodies
Melancholic melodies
Murder my motivation
How I remember
The sun comes from a

A guitar that gently weeps
I am a rockstar
In the symphony of infinity
If my song be a sad one
So be it
I will play it the best way
I can
With tears that burn
And reap what they sow
I am me
Summertime Smiles
With a heavy heart
Of snow.
Melancholic melodies
Murder my motivation
How I forget
Oh, how I forget.

At my typewriter #10 (CP)
Dogs
Sounds
People laughing
As they walk by
There are songs
I listen
Think to myself
I am too damn high.

At my typewriter #11 (CP)
I wanna be a dog in the park
Wagging my tail
Passing with the wind
Basking in the sun

All while the person I love
Colorless
In our communication
A look
A kiss upon my snout
No yesterday
No tomorrow
Just now
With you.

I can't tell if I am hurting still or where did my ethics go?
Confessions of sin
Confession
I don't know where to begin
I have been pushing
Harder than I have before
My jaw is on the floor
Dragging my feet
Out the door.
Confessions of sin
Confession
I feel lost again
Hustle to what
Hustle to win?
Hustle and thrive
Strive to live
Beyond the moment
That I die
Is that what I care about?
A legacy?
To be remembered?
wasn't there a moment
where you wanted to share

spread happiness
make people aware
of the greatness they are
they are not stuck
they are just going far
confessions of sin
confession
of something, I guess
I just know I need to speak
Get the words off my chest
But my lungs
They are filled with smoke
Of all the disbelief
All this elusive self-confidence
Hidden in doubt
Confessions of sin
Confession
I digress

At my typewriter #12 (CP)
Call it a premonition
Gut feeling
Innate correspondence
I fear the mirror
Will never show me
A beard with peppered flakes--
That my back will know
No aches
That the canes will be
Reserved for those
Who gaze at my grave
Shed tears and wonder why

This world must always take
But maybe it is just
Paranoid premonitions
One conjured
Under the indulgence
Of marijuana abundance
Rewritten ideas
Frustrated redundancy
Perhaps I just want to stay young
Even if it means
Young is my end
An end that is too early
Maybe not
Maybe I see it all
What if I really tried to see it.
An old man
An old face
With a young heart
That beats to drums
Foreign to my aging ears
Where my mind comes,
Just to fade
But when it is there
It is there
Even if I don't recognize
The face with a peppered beard.
A back that aches.

A failed writer was high on heroin and asked me for a poem about 'flattery' but left before I could finish. He was a violent and aggressive reflection of the worst version of myself.

Butter me up

Nice and fat
Destructive.
Retract. Refile. Repeat.
I find myself in strawberry fields
Rolling with Lennon
In a glimmer
Elastic and eclectic.
Butter me up
Nice and fat
The fire below my feet
Soul sweats above the heat
Butter me up
I stay
And go away
Lost in a sentence
Lost in my sentence
Butter me up
Nice and fat.
I am delightful
Butter me up
Nice and fat.
I am destructive.
I am destructive.
I will destroy you.
Butter me up
Nice and fat
Give me all the fucking lies
Tell me I am handsome
Beautiful and wise
Butter me up
Please, I beg you
I can't look at myself anymore
Not with these honest eyes.

At my typewriter #13 (CP)
Another day
Another experience
Where they replace
Spaces carved
By the destruction
Of days passed
I am not the poet
I will be
I am the poet
That slams the keys
Right now
I exist on a page
In a prose
In a poem
Afterward, I cease
I cease so that
I may turn the page
Wined my ribbon
Write new ideas
New topics
New stories
New me
The poet, at this moment
Is destined to die at the end of the page
So that he may be born into
A clean slate
A clean state that mourns
Who I once was
The poet
Tabu la rasa
Watch as I

Envelop within myself
Evolve myself
With my language
An adolescent adult
A noble savage
I am just an idiot
I am just madness

At my typewriter #14 (CP)
The sun is back!
A tickle in my spine
A breeze on my neck
Guitar rift divine
My eyes are bliss
I am mine
Whether the world cares
Whether this poem rhymes
I am back--
The sunbathes me in light.
There is a sensation in my eye
I can feel my fingers
While I type.
I smile at people,
No reminder is necessary.
I have shaken winter
I am blooming.
Farwell to myself
The one that knew me.

A Haiku

Sunlight on the wall

Shadow winds; gentle in leaves.
Crimson afternoon

Another Haiku

The wind is near me
Branches ache and yell
Red tulips tremble

One more for the road

A wordless whisper
The world of eyes tell me
Truth hidden in lies.

Revelations
Sitting by a fire.
Alone. In awe.
Allowed that to burn in my chest.
Said it was love
Because I wasn't alone.

Intelligence?
We danced to a beautiful melody.
Never heard the song
But I lead her.
She stepped and swayed.
I dipped and turned.
The song compelled me
To sing lyrics
I didn't know.
The rhythm slowed.
There was a chill in the air.

I held this beautiful woman
In strong arms.
Arms stronger than my own.
I whispered that she gave me life.
She whispered,
This song was for—
The song was for life.
Confused.
She told me she was madness.
That we were time.
Chaos and order.
My arms were weak.
Weaker than my own.
My knees trembled.
The rhythm picked up again.
I looked her in the eyes
They were withered
The hands in hers were
Tired and scared.
Our feet bled.
I stepped and swayed.
She dipped and turned.

Don't let me down
The weather plays a role.
One out of my control.
Leaving me inside.
Leaving me alone.

A novel to write
A story growing old
In the retirement home
Of my third eye.

A shitty view of things to do
That despite my
Caffeinated work-ethic
The story remains
Trapped in my brain
Wondering why it
Must be limited
To my rainy days.
Next to all the love poems
I wish I could write.
But pain grips my pen
Shoveling me in
my grave dug by might.

So on my sunny days
I can run free,
But I land in love
With eyes that hold.
Curls that are young,
Will be curls grey and old
That hopefully see
The potential man
Trapped within me.

Free as a bird.
Free as the breeze.
When the story comes out.
Don't give up on me.
When the story comes out.
Please believe.
When the story comes out.
I am just struggling
To get it out.

A shitty view of things to do
That despite my
Caffeinated work-ethic
The story remains
Trapped in my brain
Wondering why it
Must be limited
To my rainy days.
Next to all the love poems
I wish I could write.
But pain grips my pen
Shoveling me in
my grave dug by might.

So on my sunny days
I can run free,
But I land in love
With eyes that hold.
Curls that are young,
Will be curls grey and old
That hopefully see
The potential man
Trapped within me.

Free as a bird.
Free as the breeze.
When the story comes out.
Don't give up on me.
When the story comes out.
Please believe.
When the story comes out.
I am just struggling
To get it out.

I held this beautiful woman
In strong arms.
Arms stronger than my own.
I whispered that she gave me life.
She whispered,
This song was for—
The song was for life.
Confused.
She told me she was madness.
That we were time.
Chaos and order.
My arms were weak.
Weaker than my own.
My knees trembled.
The rhythm picked up again.
I looked her in the eyes
They were withered
The hands in hers were
Tired and scared.
Our feet bled.
I stepped and swayed.
She dipped and turned.

Don't let me down
The weather plays a role.
One out of my control.
Leaving me inside.
Leaving me alone.

A novel to write
A story growing old
In the retirement home
Of my third eye.

I promise it is there.
Watch how I type.
Cupping my hands
I grab the air.
Smother my face
In the pillow
Of false wind.

The deep state
Sitting in the cool comfort
Of a summer night.
Alone.
I was alone with others too.
No bother.
I closed my eyes,
This was good grass.
I wanted to meditate.
Really feel it.
The darkness swallowed me whole.
It felt right to sink,
So, I sank.
Deep into a melody.

Dragon dance.
Purple bamboo.
Flowing water.
Phoenix from fire.
Lotus out of water.
Leaves of autumn.
Jasmine flower.

My mind was untethered.
I would have forgotten my body

Yet my palms were out in front of me.

Out of my chest,
Shined a bright lantern.
Behind me was a sky before dawn.
The darkest Night.
Looking down, I saw a samurai.
He sat in seiza.
A black and white kimono.
Katana rested on top of pink orchids.

He grabbed his small blade.
He looked up at me.
Squinting squinted eyes.
I was the sun.
I was also him.
He cut his bun.
Dishonor.
The loose bun rode the wind.
He turned the dagger on himself.
A moment.
Contemplation. Doubt. Forgiveness.
Dug it deep into his belly.
Dragged the sword
From left to right.
Seppuku.
Honor.
The blade was certain
Sharp like neon lightning.
Oh, how the thunder roared.

I was the sun.
I was also him.

His body collapsed.
Pink orchids-stained red.

My fingers burned.
I jumped.

The joint had burned to nothing
In between my fingers.
Alone.
I was alone with others too.
Looked at my watch.
It was six am.
The sun was rising.

No bother.
I closed my eyes.
Brought it back to my lips.
Inhale what was left.
This was good grass.
Exhaled all I was.
I should tip my dealer.

Next time I pick up my sword.
I will spill my guts.
Honor.
A notebook filled with
Pink-orchids-stained red.

Portrait of a wandering soul
There was a painting.
Lips upon embrace.
Inches away.
Longing. Craving.

On the edge of existence.
There they were.
Knowing everything about nothing.
Nothing of everything.
He was slightly above
Tethering her to the air.
Anchored by the weight
Of their gravity.
She was floating
Slightly above it all
At the precipice of ecstasy.
Their lips repelling.
Their lips possessed.
Not a single thought
Behind the brush strokes.
Brushed strokes infused
To give us the view
Of the artist.
Who stares at a wall,
Seeing it all.
Violently removed
At the thought of
If only
We could live forever
in a moment…

This is me
GOOD MORNING!
I just wanna…
Dance! Sing!
Run in the hills.
Smoke some weed
Read a book

Have a coffee or tea
Go to work
Pay my bills…

A note from the morning before going to Central Park
Follow your instincts.
When the poem of your soul
Flows with the poetry of music.
The soul of the world.
Find it; hold it.
Trust what you've been through.
Trust what you will do.

A poem found
Sanity in sanity
Is my insanity.
Something I've seen with more dignity
But some do or die.
When do we fight to cry?
When do we fight to survive?

An ode to the countless immigrant who illuminated my privilege through their glowing resilience

When I was young
My parents hired
A reserved Ecuadorian woman.
A hundred bucks a week
Was the price for her to come and clean.
In a sweaty frenzy
Flying through the tasks.
Opening about an hour at the end of the day.

She'd sit with me.
As I struggled with my S's
Ten less three.
In her little English, she knew
She always said
One isn't as good as two.
We'd figure it out together.
She was forty less four.
At the end of the year
She'd ask
To keep the books.
She has a son she'd like to teach
Once he got here.

Went to high school with plenty.
Their world isolated
Developing their own community.
Some days I would,
I would swear to hate them.
Like I wasn't Hispanic enough
My skin is too fair.
Just because my family employed theirs.
Looking back
I never asked
If they'd like to sit
At my table filled with empty chairs.
A lot of them
Ended up in great colleges
Advanced degrees
Knew more than I could begin to see.
In better jobs
In better worlds
Established and sound.

Some of them
Ended up in the military
Immigrant-patriot was a thought
Strange to entertain.

Almost as strange
As the idea of school
Tuition. Student loans.
A lifelong career
Based on teenage fear.

So, no school for fools
Brick and mortar
Became my essays.
Pushing hard
While older generations
Whispered of
Wheel barrels that build character.

Taught myself a language.
Conversational trial and error.
But the men that surround me,
They cannot understand.
The language I speak
The opportunity I take for granted.

There was Venditto
A twenty-eight-year-old police officer
Left his son & wife
When hoping the border
Of do or die.
To come and lay some tile.
Once, I expressed my frustration.

With this country
Of capitalistic corruption
A desire to leave
And begin again.
This was the first time
In my semi-adult life
That I felt
Threatened and ashamed.
He was red in the face
When he screamed.
He wished he had
What I had.
Reminding me
Not to throw it away.
Every lunch break
Venditto would read
A copy of Huckleberry fin
Never understanding the words within.
Having to start at the beginning, again.
Never further than page ten.
Maybe better that way,
Missing out on all that southern river language.
Tomorrow would be another day.
On page one for a new trial.
Of recognizing inadequacies
And trying to get better.

There was Raul
From Peru
Aged forty-two
Who hadn't seen his boy
Since twenty-five.
His daughters were here

But it was clear
The trauma of arrival
Had left them dead inside.
Sometimes on lunch breaks
I'd call their therapist
To translate as best as I could.
Bipolar depression
Intense introspection.
The pain they experienced
Alone on their journey---
Has caused psychological regression
Repression of words
Because they have seen a world
That the girls in her class
Who tease and pull hair.
Could never imagine.
Could never know.
They have--
Not having as out of their reach.
Perpetuating a cycle
Of hate
In both directions---
One they must burry
And hide
Because they have survived
The journey into
Promised better days---
Old Raul would cry.
He'd ask why.
And I never quite
Had the answer.
To him
Our days spent together

Filled a void
Of a boy
Turned into a man.
That needed attention
A real-life boy
Grew up alone
In a place called home,
But never felt like it,
Without his Father's presence.
The guilt of it all
Was justified by Old Raul
For the opportunity
He achieved in arrival.
He let one child down
He couldn't make this mistake again.
His daughters were his redemption.

On old Raul's bad days
He'd ask me to arm wrestle
An attempt to save
Some bravado.
I'd fight back
Then submit a more muscular arm
He smiled and went back to work.
Thinking that this old man isn't done yet.
On those days, I swear I saw
Mighty Incan fight within his eyes.

When I started to work
I was seventeen.
Untrustworthy of responsibility.
Everywhere I went, I brought
Don Rio with me

He was fifty-seven then
Maybe four foot-ten
But despite the odds
He always outworked me.
He saved every penny
Sent it back home
Living like a hermit
In his rough conditions
A studio apartment for thirty-six years.
Since he had seen
His wife and children.
He retired recently
To enjoy his final years.
With the many of suffering before them.
He owns a cheese farm
Somewhere remote and hidden,
Drinks it like it is the blood of salvation.

Finally:
My parents.
Their siblings.
Came here
With fifth grade educations
To start a business
Achieve a dream; one sold
On Coca-Cola commercials.
A neighbor's radio.
From farm to front lawn
They worked all day,
All Night Long.
To give me and mines
What we needed

A bubble of what
We could - never know
A struggle ugly and unjust
So, we can start a life
In the land of opportunity
With less hate and frustration
In our veins,
Polluting our brains.
So, we wouldn't be
Ostracized
Kept outside.
But we were
By the darkness of our hair
The complexion of our skin.
The privilege we claimed to deserve.
Tastes here and there
Followed by further isolation.
For a long time
I believed in Original Sin.
Now I arise from the shadows
My scars illuminated by the experiences
Of a world.
Of what could have been.
I am angry.
I am frustrated.
I am grateful.

For her bad day
All poems of love
Are poems of you
My fingers move upon the keyboard
A rapid vigor
Nostalgic of your hips

Longing for your skin
I share pieces of this broken heart
Pieces that you showed me.
Places deep within
That I thought could only be viewed
From the lens of a nocturnal nightmare.
Things that would scurry when
Light was shined within.
But now I reflect in Central Park
Giving what you taught me to take.
I love you on your good days
On your bad days, even more.
they are a reminder
you are so much more
then all I could adore.

El Mate

Que lindo es
El Puente
Armado de muchos manos.
Que lindo es
El Puente que dejan pasar
Arriba del rio
El rio de tiempo

En mis momentos
De pobre soledad
Me toman un mate
Y tengo un companero

Visions de mi Viejo

Mi mano tapando del hueco
Preparando la yerba.
Ecos de un voz
En la distancia
Que solo pecisas ganas
El voz de mi Viejo
El sentido se mis abuelos
De mis pais

Hechando la agua
Y escucho Lluvia en el campo.
El crepitar de yerba
E crepitar de totra frita
De milenesas

Reincarnacion?
Claro que si.
Mi siento nuevo con cada sorbo.

Visions de mi viejo
De mis abuelos
De mi pais
Estoy distante
Pero con el mate
Nunca perdido

Visions de un rio
Cuatro Charrua
Sentado a lado un fuego
Harapos en el pelo negro
Sin zapatos
Con piel cansado
De un pelea con el sol

Un pelea con el dia
Pasando el mate
Abajo un-Cielo celeste
La luna colgada
De una oveja mansa

Algun dia
Voy a pasar un mate
A mis hijos
Pero estos manos
Ques escribing las poemas
No va estar
No esos manos en otro ojos
Son los manos
Que construen un Puente
El Puente que crusan
Mis viejos
Mis abuelos
Mis pais
Los cuarto charua
El gaucho cansado
Todo abajo de un
Cielo celeste
La luna colgada.
Todo arriba de
Un rio del tiempo.

Y cuando mis hijos proban
Voy a decir una cosa.

La primera es dolor
La segunda carinho
Tricera es la verdad

El cuatro es la Muerte
El quinto es el naciemento
Luego vertemos de nuevo

Y ellos vas a escuchar
Un voz en la distancia
Diciendo que
Solo precias ganas.

May-Day
This morning
The rising sun wedged its way in-between
Mine and my lady's
Lips. Lips. Lips.
A reflection in a dead television set
Shows me a head
Wind of whisper crisp
Struggling to get ahead.
Barely kept up.
Barely keeping on.
Dragging myself
Through movements of
Morning. Mourning.
Soap and hot water showers devour
This clean body from yesterday.
Coffee. Eggs.
Roll some weed.
Grab my backpack.
Two journals.
One for this.
Another for that.
Three notebooks.
School. Poetry. Philosophy.

Greek Tragedy.
Ginsberg and Whitman.
A laptop.
Covered in stickers of places
I'd rather be.
A backpack filled with fantasy.
Walk out of the apartment.
The joint between my
Lips. Lips. Lips.
Walking down the street
Before I could bring
My flames to exhale
What was that promise you made?
Touch me.
There is a mirror.
 We don't look the same.
Walking down the street
There is an ambulance
A man on a stretcher.
Two paramedic cranes
Hover over his membrane
Drilling his chest.
Pumping his face.
Get to my car
Have a break
From my mental break
Save the joint for later
The first adult decision
Of the day.

Random prose from my notebook on May 11, 2022.
   The more time I am actively living, it feels like the more justification I have that I belong nowhere. But I am alone right now in

the park. There is litter and garbage and a red flower. It is standing in front of it all. The way the moon stands in the way of the rest of it.

A train passes by, as does an Indian mustache and glimmering sunglasses. Branches always make me think of old people. With all their wrinkles and bark.

The unlit joint fell out of my mouth.

There is a flat green plain. All somewhat the same. At least to my untrained eye. But there is more to this lumpy bed of green.

A train passes by. This time heading north. A red streak cuts through a silver cylinder cloud.

The violin has stuck me. As has the mosquito. I am falling into a gentle unconsciousness. One where I make peace with the experience as it happens. The blessing-----

I don't know what it is. This slow blink of wonder welcoming me within. It feels whole-y.

The danger technology really holds. With each improvement and innovation, someone is responsible for the distribution of those benefits. These undisclosed benefits that only all could know, but only a few will say. As our capacity to interrelate languages continues to improve, countless rewrites will come—with each one slightly mingling the absolute reality. Each one is a result of the author and editor's decision. Subject to their individual biases. Subtly known or unknown.

This also leaves this system subject to abuse. Because the easiest/most effective form of manipulation are intentional accidents.

The second a word is changed in a book, it is no longer the same message. Despite the message never being the same for any two readers. But I need originality, mother fucker! Give me all the---

The train is heading southbound.

I see many people screaming the same thing through different actions.

Pain—the type of thing you sing about.

Either out loud insane in the way you insane the others. Or inside bouncing off the hollow walls; prefrontal cortex incarceration.

THE POET'S JOB IS IN THE SUN.
The novelist—the philosopher under a yellow light lamp shade, charge forward and invade the deepest shade of this black ocean.

I see out the disco ball, each square a face.
Swallowed by the dark embrace.
Or am I just projecting?
Does none of this make sense?
I could be just trying to lay my thoughts to rest.
What do I know?
I am not the best.
Regress. Try best.
Emotions to the chest.
Revisit. Reinvest.
I don't know what to say.
All I know is I look and see only places I am not meant to be.
Trying to justify it. Take this weight from me.

Random prose from my notebook May 12, 2022
These pens are more like paint brushes.
"Practice poem"
There was wind
Some sunlight too.
Breeze on my ankle.
Pushing me to move.
A warrior dance.
A warrior scream.
Is a man a river
Or just his stream
Is a man free
From all, he used to be
There was wind

Sunlight warmed my chest
Breeze at my back, forcing me to think
Pushing me to <u>move.</u>

Dump some more!
Flip flop.
Drop stop
Crip walk
Never talk
Ming ling
Chicken wing
Zip zap
Shut your trap
Lobby wobbly
My friend
Snobby bobby
Horsed purse
We put it in reverse
On this day
I tried to play
Stoic stuck
Always sick
Never happy
Flip the switch
Ooze bruise
My loving goo
All the words
Lost in you
Ooze bruise
Never know what to do
Ooze bruise
I am losing you

Poetry
Poetry. Oh, poetry
Cleanse the pollution
In my breeze.

Poetry. Oh, poetry
Have the freedom
That I need.

As the stone of my senses
Sink deeper and deeper
To the moment, I watch battling sea creatures.
Outer space aliens at war underneath.

Is this the battle
Of space and time
Of the electrons
That makes my
Capricious mind
A galactic fight
For the value assigned
By those who withheld it
Craved by those blind with best intentions
Blind. Blind. Blind.
I see a world divine.
For a woman in red.
She remains
Even after she climbs out of my bed.
Oh, poetry
Please soothe
My rotten stench.
This shaky leg.

Cracked and shattered,
Decisions outside
Of my imaginary mind.
Where to go?
What to do?
And how to say?
When do they need the truth?
Should I be the one to say it?
Oh, poetry
Please remedy me
Let me drink your words
And fill the cracks in my head.
Oh, poetry
Recover me
From my regression
Sinking into the
Waterbed of my introspection.
Oh, poetry
I tried to smoke you out
But I forgot there
Are clouds in heaven.
Oh, Poetry
Let me type
And bleed over the page
Filling the canyons within.
With the wisdom of lost age.
Let me remember
How to breathe.
Oh, poetry
Give me that and nothing more
I promise that is all I need
To decide how
I'd like to view this world.

How?
How do I tell
Someone, I don't think they are
With the right person?
How do I love myself,
When I don't get anything done without
A soul of hate?
How do I make sure I get a mortgage?
How do I pay rent?
How do I get out of debt?
How do I tell someone—

I need to be alone for a while?
That they are the only people I don't feel alone with?
It all makes me overwhelmed?
That it's not that I don't want to hang out?
That I just don't got it in me?

How do I tell them—
To back off?
To come closer?
That I am gone?
There is nothing left inside?
That I also ooze with joy?
That I hate it all?
That I don't care?
That I am okay?
That it's too much?
The walls are going to cave in?
That, never mind, I am okay again?
While I am going away?

How do I tell them—
I struggle to keep it together?
That all the soul-of-self I have misplaced haunt me?
That they haunt me
In shadows,
In reflections,
At my own heartbeat?
That some nights I can't sleep?

How do I tell them—
I was purged in the depths of my own hell?
That I built hell brick by brick?

How do I ask them—
If they are alright?
If they still care?

How do I tell them—
I still care?
That I need space?
That I am not the same?
That our versions of love,
Do they just look different?
That I am struggling to express my pain?
When I look in the mirror,
I don't feel the same?

How do I tell them—
That I still care?
That just because it is different
I still love them?
That this pain unexpressed

Is long repressed?
That this world takes too much?
That despite that
There is still a flame in my chest?

How do I tell them—
That I will protect that flame?
No matter what?
No matter the changes?
That my hope for you,
For me,
For the world,
For decency,
Is the only constant?
That hope and love and compassion
Are not going anywhere?
as long as I am around
they live within the course
of my veins?

How do I tell them—
Even when I am down,
I haven't given up?
That the world can't have my hope?
That I'd rather die than ever stop writing?
That I'd rather die than become a god?
That I see god exists in a moment,
In music, in art,
In grass, in trees,
In oceans, in the breeze,
In sunlight, in moonlight,
In beauty, in ugly,
In death, in life,

In strangers and in animals?
That I don't believe god exists?

How do I tell them—
That we always choose to walk among people?
That we always walk among people?
That there is something special about this experience?
That it needs to be cherished?
That I'd rather die,
Then lose whatever that is?
That I am scared, too?
That I'd hold your hand?

How do I tell them
That I feel alone?
How?

Know thy self

Gentle in her arch
Golden in her shimmer
Above her but ever-distant
The way she balances above the world.

Twin demons of chaos
Bound to famine and war
Shackled balefully bound to their gong
Apocalypse ripples in our heads

As I sit in the courtyard
Of a dead man from Spain
Walls sponged in dirt and love
Porcelian Pompeii; brass people crystalize the pain

Oh, the anguish of gentle stillness
Watch as my copper rusts away
Yet, the frame-my cast
Echoes in an endless river.

My soul remains.

I die

It's a serendipitous silence
The wings flutter
The river runs
A loving silence
An echo
Of empty
An echo
Of love
Bound until eternity
Finds it's voice
Until king's steal crowns
The body bent and curved
Eroded and damned
The heart fluttered
In it's threshold.
Releasing. Revealing. Revolving.

What a weird day

I met Kerouac once.
He was wearing a white and pink
Short sleeved button down.

I met Neal Cassidy once.
He stood with him
On that fateful day.
He wore Navy Blue.

A woman was dealing—
Dealing bad.
She needed a piece
Of my spirit.

I gave it away.
Told myself I had it to spare.
I always forget how deep is my grave
Of grievance and despair.

Dragging the feet belonging
To a vacuum of a man
Dampening his reeving rapture to offer
A stranger a hand

I had stepped into
An altered reality.
Lugging my craft
In the heat of summertime.
There is a young boy and girl dancing
To the song
Of a musician trying to make it.
Ask me why I'm addicted.

But there they were.
Jack and Neal.
In plain sight before me.
Walking towards them.

Jack looked at me.
I said, "Are you…"
And Neal grinned.
Jack chuckled out the side of his mouth.

"Would you like a beer kid?"
I looked down and they were splitting a pack.
I grabbed it
Shook their hands.

"Are you…"
"Thank you."
The only words I said to them
On that fateful day.

I have to stop writing this poem every time.
I just stare out my apartment window.
Watch branches sway.
Listen to Jazz.

"Would you like a beer, kid?"
I crossed the street
And watched them walk away
Laughing and hugging.

Until the back of their heads
More and more distant.
Until I take the corner
Until.

I am alive again.
There is a sweaty beer

In my grip.

I think nobody
Will believe me
My brief trip to the underworld.
But, I have this beer.

I tuck it in my bag
Later in my fridge.
Where it sits.

Waiting for the day
I publish my first book.
And I'll have a toast
With my dead friends

Oh, moon river
Please give me a kiss.
Oh, sunny day
Hold me tight.

The Grand Inquisitor

Wake up.

4

Tomorrow Will Be Yesterday

There are some things I would like to clarify on the following poem. This poem was the result of a long period of not writing for myself. I had no idea what was going to come out and I wrote in one long burst. There are things mentioned in the poem that do not align with my personal beliefs. For example there is a line that says, "stop fucking like it is a hobby". I have absolutely no problem with promiscuity. I think this is perhaps a comment on the desensitization of casual sex. Fuck as much as you can, but when you fuck then fuck. Don't fuck like you are playing cards with your friends.

There is also a line that sexualizes the black female body. Black womena are hot. So are latinas. Asian women and white women. On this particular day I wrote about black women. Maybe a black woman made eyes at me at the gym or the coffee shop or the book store. I meant nothing by it. It's insensitive and arguably racist the way it is presented, but I ain't perfect.

This poem is me digging. I see it as anescavation more than a decleration. Why I read it at Bowery still makes no sense to me. The more I saw it sitting on a folder on my book shelf (A folder that was emptied after I was living with my family and went away for a while), the more I felt drawn to read it. Almost as if performing it was a calling. Don't impose more meaning to this then necessary.

I read it and the experinece was cathartic. An emotional and spiritual unfolding. Shortly there after my life circumstances began to unfold. For that reason I have decided to add this project.

```
Art was not meantxx xx
   People aren't to impress
      Kids to cry
         Dogs in hunger


Love is not to give up
      happiness has no ownership
         Humans to tame
            hatred to divide


   my ideas are clear
         then they shape shift
            in my chest

I know everyone loves everyone
   here we go again
      maybe forgive
         that we are not always
                                       at our best
that our best is also
                  our loneliest
Art was meant
People to impress
Kids to cry
Dogs in hunger
            We have given up.
               What does this say of our
LOVE?
            I witnessed a great
               waterfall once.

            Logically
                  I looked over the
                                 edge.
         The drop was immense.
         The water roared.
         Mist flew high.
         Eye was looking
         at a tiny trickle
         its slight song dorned out
         the roar echoing inside.
```

Do speak to me with greatest charmisma.

Don't hide yourself
your face will blister.

Speak to me. Or dont speak to me at all.
I am not a short man
don't expect my patience
to be tall.

Watch as I navigate myself
in this sea of endless mirros,
    There is correspondence
       in my tragedy.
          Hope in my comedy
            is that hope?

                      I have errands to run
                      but I have misplaced my
                      sword and shield.

Good night Osiris,
Let your song provide
 Dreams OF melody.
Where you can ride the waves
 of a cloudless orgasm.
   Curly hair in your teeth
       and two dragons dancing
           in a pink morning sun.

              A volcano errupting
                sounds like thunder
                    but the floor trembles
                    with hestitant wonder.

It was a good afternoon
         according to the sea and sky.

A quetzal flew a great distance
and landed upon   the pirch piercing
                         through my chest
           Good evening,
           fair bird
           may I look you
           in the eye.
           What says you
           of the world--------------------
           of this pointless
           dreary life?
It was a good afternoon
         according to the sea and sky.
The bird
speaks in a song
that is faster heard
than understood,
but better understood
than heard.
I grew. To grow is to grow angry.

           So, I sent this colorful
           creature down my conscious
                  shoot.
           To go after the Canary
             or to see where
             she had nested
             the truth.

There were few of us left
  our president said last call.
But there were still few of us
  drunk on philosophy
  dancing to music.
Being at odds with ourselves
    barefoot in the rain
              was the truth
    but so was pneumonia.
Fuck you! Feeble finite
  falliable fiend! Forever friends
        with the devil and me,,,,

There were few of us left.
We'd read these guys
someone too   dont get me wrong
some women too
they just had less to say (what is heard)
less ways to say it!
thats what I am looking for.
Don't start fucking withme
at the first slip of my
patriarchal buck teeth.
They have always gotten in the way
of when eating forbidden fruit.
Nobody chooses
    this body
    this view
          all we can do
        is try to improve
        give people room

But there were few of us left
drunk on philosophies
dancing to music

                    writing poetry
                    with pen and paper
                    or as our eyes
                    read Dickinson
                    Heard Nina Simone
                    watched a beautiful
                    stranger put a

"An Obituary to
a dead Canary. Read
by her replacement
THE QUETZAL . Who
is also now dying."

CHIRP*chirp* CHIRP* chirpppp*
allow me to translate:

Lament my fair lady.
They not knowth what they've done.
Your lungs are blistered and boiled!
They forget to see
how these gentle wings
have been scorched
by a dying son.

Lament my fair lady.
Feel pity for your past,
for when you were here
the future came at you fast.

Chirp* chirppp!
Forgive me my fair reader.
This truth is better left
where darkness thrives;
brightness runs.

Gratitude my fair reader.
It is normal to feel angry
upon awakening.
Chirp* Chirp*
Clock in
Clock out

    Why do we debate justice?
    Brown and black people
    are dying.
    A system in place

Keeping people
idiologically trapped
in their body.
Love making is intimate
stop fucking like it's a hobbie.
Why do we debate happiness?
Women are trapped in a gaze
of a male suicidal body.
Over stimulated
and desensitized.
Emotionally unavailable
they have never seen their father
cry.
The same gaze
that tucked the mother's beauty away
now looks at her
arteries to the surface
fingers that held her hand
are now gripped with rigor mortis.
Takes that beauty
and brings it to the surface.
If you listen carefully
the falling leaf
holds her lament.

It's languid
and long
into shallow descent.

Decreped and crusted
our back can barely hold it.
As we search for the   fountain of youth
                  a moment in between
debate and sorrow.
To beg that our judgment is coming
find the information
and know it.
A new out look life, but to live itself--
we take that decision
and postpone it.

There once was a cowboy
   a snake lays eggs
   in his skull.
His Spirit is tumbleweed.

There once was a warrior.
    Their armor lasted
     longer than their teeth.
A heart etched in stone.

We were carnivorous bastards
I feel it in my bones.
Domesticated animals,
law and order-a mask of clever greed-
has whipped the backs of many
wants to forget
that we are building
a throne of
our worst deolation
our merciless misery
so that apocalypse may sit
and those with money
(if they are lucky)
will get to kiss their toes.
But when we look to the moon
we must remember
that flowers die in November
and bloom again in ~~xuuurxx~~ spring.

There was once a sailor
  he left his lady
  to go out and explore
  the sea.
Her cries fell silent
all he heard was the breeze.

 There was once a woman
 with a single breast
 she sent her heart
 in a song.
 The canary knew it best.

There once was a cowboy
   a snake lays eggs
   in his skull.
His Spirit is tumbleweed.

There once was a warrior.
   Their armor lasted
   longer than their teeth.
A heart etched in stone.

We were carnivorous bastards
I feel it in my bones.
Domesticated animals,
law and order-a mask of clever greed-
has whipped the backs of many
wants to forget
that we are building
a throne of
our worst deolation
our merciless misery
so that apocalypse may sit
and those with money
(if they are lucky)
will get to kiss their toes.
But when we look to the moon
we must remember
that flowers die in November
and bloom again in ~~xxxxxxx~~ spring.

There was once a sailor
  he left his lady
  to go out and explore
  the sea.
Her cries fell silent
all he heard was the breeze.

There was once a woman
with a single breast
she sent her heart
in a song.
The canary knew it best.

"What the canary said
to the QUETZAL, from beyond death"

We are damned by our need to protect.
A phase transition
bound within bone and breast.
Dont' forget to touch the ground.
Always try your best.

The spirit of the canary
    took it's final breath.

I saw the bird
    bursting out!
the cave was benath
the waterfall.
The waterfall
remains trapped
within my head.
The birds burst of dance
removed me from my gazing eye.
from the endless trickle
of the waterfalls silent spine.
It flew to the sky
coughing up a boiled lung.
It was only 6 pm
but I wondered if from up there
it could see a setting sun.
It danced
It danced
and only down here
did it look alone.
Mid- June
but my skin raised
at the sensation of falling snow.

When I wake
there is still whiskey
on my breath.
I cork the last gulp
of a bottle resting on the counter
next to a trap for the roaches.
I see one crawl into the toaster
and think I dont need breakfast.
I'd put the coffee on,
door open while I picked
out my outfit,
The more extravegent my presentation
the better I can hide my home.
The one where
weed and alchol numb
me enough
to tolerate myself.
Where I sit in hours of silence
visiting the gallows
of my unconscious.
Rape me.
Hate me.
Kill me.
God forbid, I ever feel free.
Talk to cock roaches when your lonely.
See glowing skin within.
Garden of earthly delights,
a skeleton is my best friend.
Off to work.
Coffee stain on my shirt.
Madness in my place of work
always made me rest assured.
Listening gave my depression
a temporary cure.
Expectations always showed
the way temporary fixes
always lead to hurt.

Art was meant
    That love is giving up.
    Happiness is yours to claim.
    In the mirror, a human face
    will always show you shame..
    That hatred is there to teach
    to forgive.
    To forgive another
    is to forgive your misunderstood
                         pain.
Art was not meant to be
              entitled bureaucracy.

    My feelings are in need
        of expressing.
    My feelings are so damn
        unclear.
    They take over my torso
        where Osiris took Apollo's arrow.
        Shot it through my vest.
        The one I hemmed myself.
        I used my grandmas cracked hands.
        For buttons, my grandfather's eyes.

  My feelings are clear
      then they shape shift
          in my mind.

 I know everyone loves everyone.
     Here we go again.
     But at the very least

       we can try.

 It was a good afternoon
     according to the sea and sky.

5

Stone Upon Stone

Poems from a year of affliction and agoraphobia; rising up. To reclaim myself as I prepared to move from my home state of New York. I never lost hope, but these poems begin from a place of crippling writer's block. Ending in a place where I believed that if I fought for others, then maybe I could fight for myself.

I was able to write my first poem since leaving the hospital about a month and a half after discharge. The longest I had gone without writing something in years. I woke up every day and grabbed a pen, but could only produce a word or two. Eventually a sentence. Then I put together a poem. Once I did that it was about keeping a habit. What really broke down the wall was I translated two or three poems by Borges into English.

What got me through it was obsessively studying aesthetics. A psychological result of these studies is that I became even more enthralled with a divine woman. She is no single person. Rather she is a piece of beauty that I have witnessed in every woman I have ever known. She is divine because she goes beyond human capacity. She is my ideal. An abstraction so deeply ingrained in literature and nostalgia that she has become an unachievable longing. She is all the good my body has ever got to experience. She is freedom and my longing for her has turned me into hope.

She saved me, but now she ruins me. In that respect she has much in common with those I used to know.

Untitled #1
Mourning in morning
Move my pen
And die.

Morning in mourning
I breathe and can
Almost fly.

To new places; sounds.
All of it can be fresh
And new.
The same old you.
The same old blue.
Good mourning!

Untitled #2
Summer rain
Creeps in like dawn.
Energy settles
And washes away.

Untitled #3

A car…
A car with subwoofers…
Maybe a truck…
Maybe a big truck…
Birds to the front right.

Birds to the back left.
One. Two. One. Two.
One, two, three. One, two, three, four.
Running water.
Not a river.
Just running water.
Like a small stream.
Or a big rain gutter.
My mom is upstairs.
She is talking loudly on the phone,
About how the dogs are needy.

A Poem About Love
At it's best
It's unconditional.
A warm welcome at the door.
Coffee in the morning?
Skin to skin.
Heart to heart.

A Poem About Passing Days
Wake and there it goes.
Setting sun
After setting sun.
Disappearing.
Sand through fingers.

A Poem About Loneliness
Walking in this state

Guarantees that my feet
Won't fire.
A solitary tattoo
On a scarred leg.
A single rose
In a scattered bush.
Splattered paint
Blocked by an isolated
Pale square.

All is diffused
By my sadness.

Untitled #4
When and why
Exhale the lungs
Yesterday is right now
Phosphorescence is my essence.
Teetering between presence
And transcendence.
Dreams of falling teeth,
Miss me with the dentist.
Do you know the way your pain?
Cut me open?
Do you know the ways?
You walk away
When I start confessing?

Crash. Break. Fall. Escape.
Dead. Love. Kiss me with your rape.
Holding all your hate.
Trying to know my fate.

Garbage dragged to the street.
Loathe the way she slaps her feet.
Scrape away the hate.
My steam is getting streamed.
Guilty what the mirror deems.
Eyes closing the story on dreams.
Heart closing to horny feens.
Mind closed to personality memes.
If only I said,
What I fucking mean.

Untitled #5
Dirty finger nails
Hair behind the ear
Messy pony tail
Head rains
Heart hails
A bug in the eye
Wind woman walks
Right on by
Palms bubbling
Stomach shakes
A smile that forgets the day
Water against rocks
A beam negates the cloud
He doesn't get my art
But he tells me that he is proud
All I hear is belief
All I see is doubt
Reel it in. Take a picture.
My brother caught a trout.
Your style is changing.
Dario, can you tell us

What your poem is about?

Untitled #6
Tomorrow, I'll walk backwards
Into yesterday
To be present with my feelings now.

Yesterday, I'll walk forward
Into whatever is next.
Gentle flower; thunder
Purple rein.

The poetic agoraphobic / Trapped in the basement of an ivory tower
    Demonstrate a conviction
    Upon linen benevolent phrase.
    Entwine a beaker of magnificence
    Dividing the underexposed.
    The shadow of your name.
    Hide and fortify;
    Precariously alone.
    If only they could see the shine
    Of your internal throne.

Untitled #7
Doom;
Zoom in on a pink moon.
It was never in the room.

Me or Her

(I must allow myself to indulge in some boastful egotism from time to time. A side effect of greatness and consistently invalid.)
Taking breathers---
Gasping between heaters
Walk it as I teach her.
Said she loves me,
But I know I can't believe her.
Said she loves me;
Can't allow myself to believe her.
Said she loves me,
If only I could see her.
Taking breathers---
Gasping between heaters
This pain in my shirt
I can't even feel hurt.

Untitled #8
Presence and transcendence
This rope is thin.
Genius and madness
This rope is thin.
It's around my throat
This rope is thin.
Hurt in my shirt
Don't know where to begin.
Palms to her cheeks----
Palm to the sky---
New beginnings.
I am the answer
But I wonder why.

Entry
Door opens
Push pull.
Boarding pass and ticket please.
Where the fuck is my wallet?

Prominence
Birds singing to each other.
Can't communicate,
But I understand. Or I think I do.
They know of my fantasies?
Yesterday's lovers.
Missed opportunities.
Forgotten books
And lingering poetry.
Devotions, causes, achievements, and triumphs.
Infidelity, effects, regrets, and defeats.

They know the way I long to sign a novel
With my name printed on the front?
To walk into an open mic
And hear whispers of legendary rumor?
Do they know the truth?
To know anything
Is to know yourself?
To know anything
Is to know nothing at all?
To know. To be. I am.
Why stand tall with a slouched ego?
Why be proud when the child cries?

Do the birds know me

For where I've been
And what I've done?
Or do they know me
From where I haven't been
And what I will do?

Then I remember.
It is just a song.
Just a walk.

Untitled #9
    A blonde smile
     Somewhere in the forgotten distance
     A sweet death
     Like honey due.
     Do not tease me
     With half bargains
     Of love and heart break.

Untitled #10
Oar in the ocean
 Moving forward
 Moving backwards
 Perspective direction
 Exterior introspection
 She hurt me with her smile
 I told her I never felt it.

Untitled #11
Exalting heat

Beneath the feet
Began to run
Never retreat
Falling gentle
Tree losing leaf
Hickory horizon
Through a storm
I once felt love
Memories adorned

Untitled #12

How many memories---

How many poems of love
Are written in these dark rooms?
Love that holds
Like the heat of June
When you say her name
Faint and swoon
If only the darkness
Contained the pain
Of fireworks colorful boom.

I split the painting
Right down the middle
Soundless poetry
My heart's gone crippled

Pink September memories
Of lilac detergent hugs.
Words of passion, but

Where is the invisible touch of love.
I want to hold it.
Water it.
Raise it to new heights.
Your lips to mine
Let the soul take flight.

Palestinian Woman in the Park
Set myself ablaze
As the path begins to narrow.
At the end of the road---
Her pretty was pious.
Olive skin; plush lips.
Gold bands on her arm.
Gold bands on her wrist.
White everything.
Red rope around her waist.
Lonely eyes,
Does she see the beauty,
Living on her face?
Don't promise me tomorrow,
All I need is right now.
I'll forgive tomorrow
If forever is allowed.
Don't promise me a minor fever
Eternal sickness is upon us now.
Give me the valley
And I will show you the mount.
Love me out loud.
Sing a song.
Paint a picture.
Swim in the river.

Dance to my music,
I'll learn the choreography of your
Sorrow; of your pleasure.
When our palms meet
I forget that I will die
The moment is infinite
Beneath the chandelier in the sky.

Pistachio / Fragments from my childhood
Punch me in the face
Don't worry I'll punch you back
The world is tough; it'll make you strong.
I'll always have your back.

Untitled #13
Whispering blacktop
We speak through dragging feet.
Tired and lonesome
Yet this spirit knows no defeat.
A perpetual state
of rising suns; walking slowly.
My spirit runs; if only you would hold me.

Untitled #14
Been searching for love
But my poetry is rigid.

Up is down.
Down is up.

Are you down
To see what's up?

Do you see my point?

Untitled #15
Consciousness corrupted
By capitalistic conspiracy.
FREEDOM all caps.
Price tag; small font on the back.
Resisting being sold a cog in a machine
Is an ideal sold…by the machine.

Why are there so many different
Liberation movements
Associated with the reconstruction of individual identity?
Will we never reclaim national identity?
Or patriotism that goes beyond
Warfare, beercans to forehead, and chanting with strangers
Until each sub category of a larger society that
Is filled and expanded by the individuals
Sense of self derived from an intimate,
Subjective, and thoroughgoingly valid claim
To the complex relationship we develop
With our love and suffering
As a result of the circumstances we born into
And that we develop our sense of character
And morality around, has their own
Revolution.
Not a revolution of violence,
But one in which through radical change
To quickly extinguish the flames of hate

Derived from a lack of understanding and distance
By the great oceans of love that we come to learn and understand
Though...
ART, MUSIC, CONVERSATION (WITH OUR WORDS AND OUR BODIES).
Is this a poem, anymore?
Either way I'm always just shooting the shit.

Another lap completed
My soul never depleted
I have learned to
Never be concerned
By the opinions of the conceited
May the good of this life
Be repeated.
Happy birthday.

Untitled #16
Aching knee
In midsummer dawn
Creaking lamenting steps
To a mildew of endless
Possibilities
To liberate
To dine
To divide

This is a poem about eating pussy
Love like sticky syrup
 Spread you across my day

Lick my lips
Suck on my fingers
Sweet marmalade drip down my face.
I've seen it shimmer in the eye
But I now know the flavor of your pleasure.
See the taste in your eyes
As we cum together.

The Final Line
Lead like rolling tumbleweed
  Fallen from dying tree; my heart.
  Forgotten song of loneliness.
  Silence for the fallen.
  Savory is the crunch
  Of fallen leaves beneath
  Spring footed dancing beat.
  Forgotten hymns of triumph.
  And defeat.

Doubting myself again
Good is my intention,
  But all it feels like is,
  IAMNEVERGOODENOUGH.
  I can never fill this
  Infinite jar with enough worth
  To invalidate all the invalidation.
  Diagnosis were just a word,
  Now I know they can be
  A run-on prison sentences.
  If life was as good
  As I intend it to be….

I'd....
Go to the coffee shop.
Walk my dog.
Spend hours on hours writing.
Maybe life isn't that bad.
And it is I who is the problem.

Untitled #17
In the sunny side of yesterday's...
Is where I lock myself away.
When the last bit of my imagination
Is dried up and decrepit,
Where will the flames of my being
Reside?
Will it die in empty promises?
Will it live in sidewalks below?
Dancing feet. Dancing feet. Dancing feet.
Dragging too and foe.
Under yesterday's moonlight
I brought her lips to mine.
Yes, yesterday is in the past.
Where the poet lives
And dies.
Presence is not a luxury
For those who narrate existence
As it unfolds.
The moments pass in a word.
The minutes in the prose.
The hour is your essay.

Burn me alive!

Untitled #18

I die for the immigrants in cages.
I die for those on strike.
I die for my friends.
I die for my family.
I die for my mom.
I die for my father.
I die for the dogs.
I die for orwell.
I die for Spinoza.
I die for Kerouac.
I die for Ginsberg.
I die for Borges.
I die for Bolano.
I die for Vonnegut.
I die for our Ozone layer.
I die for rotten politics.
I die for yoga and geometry.
I die for seated cockroaches.
I die for soccer.
I die for the countries that I am from.
I die for the countries that I do not know that I am from.
I die for ham and cheese sandwiches.
I die for the lettuce tomato and mayo.
I did die.
Now I die for myself.
I die to be reborn inside.

Untitled #19

I have been told my miracles were actually
Just psychosis.

Did I push myself this far
Or is this the furthest reaches
Of modern tragedy.
Young people are desperate…

If you are part of the community of people
Who have failed at killing yourself,
Then you've lost hope.
And you have found it again.
Right when it was darkest
The lights turned on again.
It was always there
Dwindling in the deepest
Recesses of your soul.
Ah, the soul!
The truest human condition
Is not knowing what to do
Toward the mystery of yourself.
The truest societal condition
Is not having room
For people to flourish
Outside the game.
Damn! I just lost.
It costs spiritual flourishing.
Not ecstasy,
Intimacy of the self.

An American Goldfinch
Lands on my tree.
The neighbor waves
As he walks by,
"nice weather we are having.",
He says.

I think,
It's become difficult to tell
What is real and what is
Psychosis.

Seeing your ex again
And my ancient hand
Rested that yellow rose
On a scarred casket.
I want to feel something.

Maybe I feel something,
I just thought it would feel different.

Empty amongst emptiness
Good bye
And memories have wrinkles
As I grow older.

Push forward
That's my little soldier
I'll make you proud
As I grow closer.

To loved and lovers,
Never surrender
Those frozen moments.
Fleeting passions
We could hold
For just one more second.

A trembling ache,

Hear the words pour through
In the way of swaying emotions.
I'm here.
With you I am where I was.
Syllables like a skipping rock
Tapping the water just enough.

Won't you lament
As I play my sad fiddle.
Nothing I can change,
Love sick skip and ripple.
I will always love her,
More than she loves herself.

Untitled #20
Cold table top
Am I, When I'm not?
Warm tea; free to be.

In the distance:
It belongs.
I become.

I begged for forgiveness
And that golden voice
Hugged me once more
"You were always forgiven".

Warm tea; free to be.
Where does the guilt come from?
My family asks if I am coming for dinner,
Maybe I am just not meant to be a writer.

A Portuguese Storm
Abandoned pier
On ferocious loneliness; my heart.
I see the stones
Holding their own,
Upon crashing erosive conformity.
Violent sea; superior unknown.
We are intimate, but I long to be you.
Gazing deep upon the horizon.
Deeper and harder.
Harder and deeper.
As deep and hard
As the ocean's unforgiving wrath.
Will I see home?
  Will I see a love abandoned?
  Upon this abandoned pier.

Bom Jesus
 As I enter the cave
 Of my imagination,
 I hear the slow trickle of water;
 Melting icicles of stone.
 Pierce from above,
 In the holes of my isolation
 At the top of silent labor;
 A sparkling city below.
 I do not speak their language.
 My tongue only utters that of
 This cave.

Solitude among spinney silent salvation.
Panacea to my pain.

Vigo
Peppers of clay roofs
Across a bay
In the palate of a northern foreign mountain side.
The current of the bay
Flows east.
The current of the bay
Flows west.

Untitled in Europe
The paradox is simple
As my horizon's expand
I only feel how small I am.

There exists an ocean
Between me and
What I know
It is only with distance
Do I finally see;
I am my own greatest foe.

Grief is not the pain
Of loss.
It is the hurt from blending
One from two.
Their pulse is gone,
But the memories are

Forever with you.

Untitled #21
She was there
    In a naked moon.
Her eyes met mine
    My passion monsoon.
She gave me love
    But I was doomed.
Super market sunflowers;
    Our eyes met.
I swear I was chosen
    Our eyes met.
Stood their frozen---
Don't go,
    But go quicker.
Every minute
    My soul grows thicker.
You are forgotten
I am forgotten.
We are lost
    My love is chained.
Street lights
    Last night
        One fight
            I'm wrong
                You're right
                Many deaths
                Only one life
Please just hold me
At least for tonight.

Fragments from the Psychiatric Unit

Barefoot in yesterday's sun
Demands flight
But these legs only know run.
To where?
Demands fight
But these hands only know love.
For what?

White doors
All the way in the back
Walk through; each time
A different past.
My thoughts are slow,
But time is fast.

Why won't Harley answer my texts?
Where her love should be,
There are only nightmares of rubber hands.

I am free falling, but
I am not looking down.
I will meet the ground,
But until then my spirit is brown.

Wake up in a sweat.
Capitan, the spirit of the hound
Tells me to kill he who holds the leash.
Wake up in a sweat.
There pierce from the doctor's glasses.
Tells me to kill who holds the leash.
Wake up in a sweat.

The doors open in the middle of the night.
The silence tells me to kill
He who holds the leash.

I can barely kill myself.

Untitled #22
Prison blue
 Tell me truth
 Dry lips
 Cracked tooth
 Hands broken
 Eyes are proof
 Stop myself
 Do what I can do
 Split ends
 Wood boards
 Devil's bend
 Spirit detour
 Hug a friend
 Kiss a hand
 Lose myself
 To find who I am
 Again.

Let the sun dry your tears
My heart; a haiku.
 My heart; a pasture.
 My heart; an ocean.
 My heart.

Best read by you.
Best walked by you.
Best swam in by you.
You.

My love is burning.
My love is frozen.
My love is dwindling.
Do you feel it?

Does it burn your lips?
Are your fingers cold?
Make sure you look up.
Do you see my misery?

If only you could know
How empty is this palace?
How cold is this conscious dome?
If only I could make you feel
What I feel…

And we go?
The song ends.
We hold each other
There was something;
Now things are different.

The Day I Found Out I Might Be Neo to My Own Matrix

Don't you know it's borrowed

Lace shirt with blue bra

Design pressing through.

Frozen lightening. Trapped in
The landscape of black & white;
A storm.

Migrant workers trimming leaves.
Cowboys in the foreground allowing
Their horses to drink cool cool water;
A hot day.

An everything white church
In a nowhere green landscape.
A family bathing in the river;
The bank is dirt and dry;
A single tree of citrus.

Moaning in a museum.
The fine art makes them cum.

I am an image;
I am trouble.
Gotta scram.

A chrome mosaic
Of explosive noodles;
Military industrial complex.

An akimbo native
With purple hair; copper skin.
A killer look.
A look with revolvers.

What are the designs to
The plastic person.
Realistic or idealistic?

My reflection in Blue;
Rothko.

I was beige;
You cut me open.

Falling down the
Stairs of despair
Into a pond of loneliness;
A koi fish falls into my mouth.

I threw up my pain;
The colors were a rainbow.

Trauma etched in concrete.
Once wet,
Now dry.
Walk all over it.
Let it catch your eye.

Always a naked dance;
Clasped fingers;
Sweaty palms.

Don't you know it is borrowed
Scrape on my knee---
 Shins; growing pains---

Ink in flesh---
Shave my head---
Do some push-ups---
Run through the woods---
Drink tequila---
Drink beer---
Drink vodka—
Run on the beach---
Fuck her---
How do you make an old fashion?
Drink some bourbon---
Punch a wall---
Drink Margaritas---
Dance---
Punch a car---
Do some pull ups---
Punch a tree---
Cut your skin---
Ink to skin---
Take some pills---
Ink to skin---
Do some sit ups—
Give up---
Cry…
Why the fuck are you crying
In the supermarket?
Pick yourself up---
Actually, give up---
You know what.
Give it one more try.
The next time you want to give up
All the times you didn't
Becomes your reason why.

Lace Shirt
Cheap mattress.
Cheaper comforter.
Pillows like nothing there.
Exhale into the atmosphere.
The one I can't recognize I'm in.

Dimly lit.
Against beige walls.
Beiger than the beige carpet.
She turns to me.
Hair up. Red lips. She is.

"How come you never
Buy me nice shit?"
As she tweezes the cig
From my fingers.

I follow the smoke
From the top of the eruption
Through her stained teeth.
Down her throat.
Into the valley of her collar bone.
The smoke is in her lungs now.
I exhale.

A navy-blue mandala
Of twists and turns
Where I imagine perched nipples
Are avalanched
By lace and cotton.

Untitled #23
Sunken serendipity
Heart gently churches
October day

Untitled #24
Sea of ideas
Bitter sweet
From the lonely island
Of the self.

My memories to eat.
Characters to debate.
But sometimes I wish
I could throw up the snakes.
Extract the gold from my spine.
Weave them together
Like a rope
Just to lasso the moon.

Either pull her toward me
Or I toward her.
Would I be able to tell
The difference?
One lonely island for another.
And another. Another.

There it is!
I forgot I misplaced it.

Don't Look Back
Bad news; Bad news.
Came and awoke me
In my sleep.

It's absurd; it's uncertain.
Rain above; rain below.
Lips like clouds in a setting sun.

The times are changing
And I don't know what's going on.
Holding on while trying to leap the hurdles.

Grandpa stole potatoes
Dad fought for his family
And it's all so...
It's absurd; it's uncertain.

Orange suede
Hugs my body.

Where is my flute?
I'm not done fluttering.

It's a breathless
Breath that reaches
To things you could never have
Or had and have lost.

Paint me forward.
Paint me backward.

What must we do
To feel all the color?
In this world of grey-blue.

The neighbor. The cat.
The dog. The wood. The meat.
The grass. The great big sea.
The mirror. All of me for free.
And when the joy is
Supposed to come.
And fill my lungs.
With all your love.
Why then, and only then
When the river runs
Through all it's bends.
All it ever is; is grey blue.

Desperate for time and all I
Ever do is waste it.
My body lays resting
I live in syllables and lines

A watercolor week
To feel my footsteps
Like brushstrokes

That's all it would take
For me to fight the good fight.
Stand up and shout
With the many
And dance with a few.
When things are untied
Take a moment to get

The knot right.
Straighten a painting
When it's tilted.
Unless it's worth more
Than you could chew.

Damn-you. Grey-blue!
Damn.
You're like snow
Frosted on the sedan
You've got work in twenty.
The manger is on your
Ass for being late.
The seconds pass by
In a frozen summersault.
Each impeding moment is
Jeopardizing your means
Of survival.
Should I just run?

The fucking defrost
Is violently fucking with
My future.
Punch the mirror.

That's you grey blue.
The frustration.
The off hand / on hand remarks.

Why are we awake to hate,
But asleep to ourselves?
The question sinks to the depths
Of my heart.

I carry the question
And the answer,
But no conviction.
It's a release.
A heard surrender.
Ebbing into your sorrow
With forgiveness and gratitude.
So, the next wave may come.
Washing you away
And for that moment
Your declaration to the passage of time
Is that you are wet sand.
Wanting so badly to come together
When the only option
Is to fall apart.
To become entranced
By the continual cycle
Of becoming and unfolding.

Why then do I choose….
That lonely color of
Grey-blue.

Acceptance. Radical acceptance.
Go! Run through that wall
In the strength of endless love.

Hike the mountains
Within and without.

Until your legs are heavy
And your toes have turned to blue.

What happens when
The chariot crashes
Into the cave.
All the paintings set to flame.

Where will the memories go
As I crawl cautiously
Down the spiral staircase
Of my shadow?
Time is moving,
But it is always midnight here.
You know that, but you can't
Shake the feeling the sunrise
Is coming.

Descend. Descend. Descend.
Finally, we arrive at the camp fire.
A younger me sitting by
The fire and looking at the stars.

Behind him a hallway
With a window
At the end.
Outside the window
Trees are shaking in the wind.

I forget how possible
Is the probable
And how probable is the possible.

I look for some
Sort of guidance

Just to retreat into myself.

The only thing I fear more
Than being misunderstood
Is being accepted.

Bad; bad news.
Came and woke me
In my sleep.

You are not tired.
You are just hungry.
This ivory palace
Is often lonely.
I fear people will know me
Before I know me.

Start before you are ready.
Tell your friends you love them
When you can.
Teach a kid something new.
Be patient with your truth.

A sleeping cyclops
Is drunk on milk and honey.
The lion fell asleep on it's back.
An island and the moon
Are tethered by sight.

I am not tired;
I am hungry.

If I don't see you

Good afternoon,
Good evening,
And good night.

6

Hope at Highest Point

have written a book at an arrogantly young age. Why I would ever presume to have the adequate means to be an authority on any sort of opinion at the ripe age of twenty eight feels like it only exemplifies the depths of my immaturity. I did so inadvertently, for writing was a mechanism of survival that transitioned into a profound gift. I do not think I am special in any way. I just coped this way for long enough and without warning I was an individual with content, a platform, and voice. At the risk of sounding even more self indulgent than what I have already outwardly presented, I'd like to dedicate this section of the poetry collection to myself.

The only way I can adequately do so is by acknowledging the people of my past who provided me support throughout the years. There are many aspects of our relationships in which I have been wronged. Though you do not seek reconciliation through accountability, I offer you an extension of grace. Not to make amends and return to the way things were, but at the very least an olive branch. What that looks like for me is thanking you all for making me who I am. For better or for worse, you have all influenced me on my journey to self-advocate and become. With that being said, when I can look past the pain of all the deceit and betrayal, I can remove the hurt from your dishonesty from some truly beautiful memories. I refuse to allow my mistreatment tarnish the wonder that this life has provided me. Even if it was a naive wonder, it was wonder and love nonetheless.

So, this section of the poetry collection---poems typed up from a light blue journal that shook up the fly's nest. A celeste journal that has a promissory note inscribed on the inside cover to, "new beginnings", is for hope. It is what drives me. Motivates me. And creates the compulsion to fight a losing battle. That battle is to be free. To be free is to be oneself absent ridicule, oppression, or abuse. I have aligned so deeply with this hopeful ideal that I no longer recognize my identity as a past that I carry, but a future I am embracing.

By extension this section being dedicated to me also means I must acknowledge that it is dedicated to you. The reader, my family, my friends, my hometown, my trauma, my triumphs, my teachers, my classmates, my culture, and the great wondrous city of New York.

I'd also like to thank my new home. I am very rough around the edges. I am not easy to love. I am eccentric and hard to pin down. I want to help, but refuse to help anyway that doesn't align with myself. I do not like sharing my intentions, explaining decisions, or letting people know my next move. I would like to thank this mysterious venture and all of it's occupants for in the few months I have lived here you have all provided me more grace, patience, and empowerment than I have experienced in the entirety of my life. It may not seem like that by my gratitude for this city and the cocktail of culture that is The Mighty Tennessee is boundless.

By extension I must dedicate this section to the haters. For without you my sheer will to not to give up would be empty. For without you the silence that hushes the open mic stage would not be so serene.

Make me the fool. Make me the meme.

I. Know. Who. I. Am.

with love,
ruben. A pioneer.

Hide and Seek Haiku

They don't know
>   It's been misplaced
Never gone.

I never took you for a man who was bothered by the wind

Wind chimes in the rain–
Naked trees creek—
Purple runs through your veins.
You feel; what you seek—

Used to wonder;
When did wondering become bad?

Clandestine clarity behind clear obscurity.
Fantastical sight; light in the dark of night.
Eyes drowning in a swan's pond.

Everything makes sense.
In the way that things don't make sense.

A warmth like no other.
Broken birds go beyond the fence.

Kinsugi lotus yesterday.
Carry it gently;
Darkness likes to play.

Hold it. Her. Him. Then.
Let them in.
They are everywhere.
Sweet nectar of existence.

Colorful and symphonic—
Lick the blood from the rose's prick.
A thick blanket into
The frigid night.
Butterflies on lonely day.
Wanderer with a tick.
A wave upon it's sway.

A red cardinal lands on your typewriter.
The ground becomes one with the sky.
She flies away.

Until next time, my sweet death.
Lips that will long for your taste.

A hard day;
You declare it to be over.
And it is over.
You are victorious.

A delicious madness
Pours it's recipe all over you.
You are baked into a cake that tastes like:
I want to keep living.
I'll go on. I'll go on. I'll go on.

Is it a lullaby
Or a psalm?

(A NOTE FOR THE READER: I'm him (them); but not HIM. Don't impose more meaning to my poetry than necessary. I am a spiritual amateur and a conduit of change. I am trying to be responsible with my platform and express abstraction. I am no savior. I can barely save myself.)

A Sublime Gratitude

I've witnessed my reflection.
Mirrors and cameras.
In a literal sense.
I see what everyone else does.

But in the silence
Of twinkling stars and silhouetted mountains.
I am.
Scattered smoke and still water.

There—I am.
Ascending toward nothing.
There—I am.
Entranced by the whisper of everything.

Here—I am.
A solid being experiencing
Experience in all of it's fluidity.

Sorrow feels the realest.
A close second is joy.
Neither one is cheap.

This morning I made tea.
As the steam-flower rose.
Eye thought about how the best meals
I've had were when I was my hungriest.

Lost in it—

I dropped my mug.
While cleaning a scattered mosaic
And boiling leaf water.
I thought.
There. Here. It goes.

An old stranger
Told me that they
Dedicated their life
To figuring out who they were.
Fulfilling and rich;
Peppered with bliss and hardship.
Only to discover
That they were never
Anything more than a
Reflection with recollection.

A golden presence
Kissed my forehead with my mother's lips.

From the cavernous
Of my identity
An ascending whisper—
Like a zero-gravity waterfall.

The flames of my heart were settled
By the voice of my grandmothers.
Their mothers; Their grandmothers.
Harmonizing—
Infinity harmonizing
in the echoes of infinitum.

"Be still.
A sublime gratitude approaches.
It is here to let you
Know that you have been
Forgiven—-

That you always were."

And at the taste of gratitude's color
I accept.
I am not unique.

I am a solid being
Experiencing experience
In all of it's fluidity.

Standing at the edge of oblivion.
Staring down the absolute.
A defiant declaration of the paradox that
I am.
One of one.
A variety of the same.

A radical of nothingness.
That contains a mason jar
Of everything.

La Duena De Mi Existencia

Besando sus lavios
Es para conocer el oblivion
Y nunca quise hacer perdido

Pero ahora
Con los pulmones lleno
De obscuridad —- me encuentran algo.
Algo, no entiendo.
No es el carino
Que me da luz,
En la sombra de mi soledad
Es el carino tullo—
Como si vos lo invitaron
La palabra
Con sus besos
Con sus abrazos
Con su presencia
El unico opcion
Es pa tener un compulsion
De aceptar
Todo y nada
Arriba del cielo
Hay que aceptar
La locura que siento adentro
Cuando su mano esta lejo
La musica que escucho
Cuando miras a mis ojos
Hay momentos
Cuando estoy solo—-
Nadando en memorias.
Respirando nostalgia.
Pienso. Estoy feliz.
Para hacer vivo.
Nada mas. Nada meno.

La luna esta colgada
En el cielo celeste—

Veo su cara.

Painfully Ordinary

The tranquil tactician
Whispers all you need
Is will—-

So I gave it—-
All. Until the only
Will left to give
Was….

Don't you understand?
    The poetry.
    The love.
    The music.
    The lines.
    Between them.
It made a believer
    Out of the embodiment of doubt.

Believing it so strongly
And when I look back
I have a sense that
    I never knew what I was doing.

I said fuck you
    To the world
    And resisted conformity
    Until it broke me.

Shattered. Crashed. Fractured.
Vanquished. Overpowered.
Dejected. Discouraged. Demoralized.
Busted. Ruined. Wrecked.
Down and Out. Disconnected.

I have a sense that
      I never knew what I was doing.

Fuck you to the world!
Resisting conformity as a moral
                          Obligation.
Until……………………….

There was a part of me
That really wanted that.

To be destroyed.
In some odd way
Validating my insistent need
To be different.
Only to realize…

I am not different.

It's Just A Shadow You See That He Is Chasing

Dad was a poor man
Now he's a rich man
Forgot what it's like to have lungs
                Like hot sand—-

Droplets bend upon
        The cherry tree.
Look at it.
Everything ever felt—
Ever loved—
Ever known—
Suspended in this droplet.

Dad was a poor man
Now he's a rich man
Forgot what it's like to have lungs
                Like hot sand—-

Pour the tea;
        follow the steam rising.
What if the mug
Was nestled in the darkest cave?
Follow the vapor.
Does it lead somewhere
Or do we too become vapor?

Dad was a poor man
Now he's a rich man
Forgot what it's like to have lungs
                Like hot sand—-

My legs are growing tired—
My spirit is weary—
All I've seen is fog—
        On the horizon.
We've been hiking for hours.
She said she "loved me".

I thought "I don't love myself…"
How strange? —-

She has altitude sickness. The rain is coming down harder by the minute.

Dad was a poor man
Now he's a rich man
Forgot what it's like to have lungs
                Like hot sand—-

Medication is on
      Their way.
They were in a different bag.
Darker by the second.
Rain is pouring.
Risk of mudslide.
      Nowhere. For. Me. To. Hide….
Chaos. Lavender and lotus blossoms too.

I held her as she
      Shivered.
Listening to the cries
Of everyone in our group.

Dad was a poor man
Now he's a rich man
Forgot what it's like to have lungs
                Like hot sand—-

WE USED TO DRINK
    BEER AND SMOKE BY THE RIVER!
  On ambitious nights

We'd hop the tracks—
Throw stones at the mountains
      And watch them land in the water.
We would curse at that
      Perpetually endless movement.
Fixing our eyes
      And watching it pass on by.
"YOU CAN HAVE US LATER,
      BUT NOT RIGHT NOW!"

Dad was a poor man
Now he's a rich man
Forgot what it's like to have lungs
      Like hot sand—-

"Hey, man", said the young beat kid
Standing next to
His fried friend.

"Sup", I said.
"You look like the exact
Kind of guy to do
Mushrooms with strangers."
, he said.
I looked at my typewriter—
I looked at them—
At my typewriter—
Them once more—

Dad was a poor man
Now he's a rich man
Forgot what it's like to have lungs
      Like hot sand—-

I'm at the MET to write.
Poems about the art.
Not describing them,
But describing the impact.
Of specific sentimentality
Something sublimely slips up my spine.

At the Egyptian exhibit.
The Temple of Dendur.
Sitting on the marble bank
of the not so nile.

There were a group
Of girls to my left.
I caught the girl at
The ending staring.
As I try to figure out this poem
about the goddess Qadesh.

At some point I have to
Acknowledge the stare.
She made me feel as if
I was the only person there.

Once I do, she uncrosses
Her legs. Revealing the
Color of her underwear
Beneath her skirt.

She saw me looking. Smiled.
A restrained chuckle.
She left with her friends.

I finished my poem.
I thought that was…
Awfully kind of her.

Dad was a poor man
Now he's a rich man
Forgot what it's like to have lungs
                Like hot sand—-

The resistance is here.
Wield your weapons with honor!
Here come the demons, witches,
Gargoyles, and giants!
Fight conformity until you collapse
       From exhaustion!
Then fight some more!
We are Knights of the Self!
The liberators of
       Mental slavery.
The poet's are the prophets of
       True progress!

Dad was a poor man
Now he's a rich man
Forgot what it's like to have lungs
                Like hot sand—-

There was a stillness
In the way he raked.
I laid the stones and watched from the side.
Tap. Tapping. Tapped.
His left forearm tightening as he reached out.
I can see the valley in his grip.

His right bicep rising like a pulse
as he and the sand became one.
Puling it in closer.
He smiled my way.

I ran to the truck to write a poem
About how being touched
Makes me want to throw up.

He whispered that I had
Come a long way.
But it was still closed.
It was a word I had never heard
One with no search results.

"Anda por sud america
Y abrir la."
I was an unnatural woman
Amidst sun kissed skin
And man's work.
Do you hear the humming within?

Dad was a poor man
Now he's a rich man
Forgot what it's like to have lungs
                Like hot sand—-

My grandma used to say
If you have a voice
Than scream for
Those who don't.

I agree with the sentiment,

But if you want people to listen
                        You've got to learn to whisper.

Dad was a poor man
Now he's a rich man
Forgot what it's like to have lungs
                Like hot sand—-

Dad was a poor man
Now he's a rich man
Forgot what it's like to have lungs
                Like hot sand—-

The two kids got freaked out
When a priest came
Requesting a poem
About world peace.

They said, "Nah, no new
People.". I understood
      Completely.

Typewriters are unique
      Machines.
Each one has it's own
Rhythm.
Too slow—the ink won't press.
Too fast—things get jammed up.

You gotta find it.
Align yourself with it.
And get lost.

When you find it…..
People gravitate.
All of sudden
There is a line
And a crowd of expectations.

My only option is to die.
Shaving off a piece
Of ego with each word written.

But it was worth it…
There has never been
 Anything more worth it.
As I repeatedly died
 And was reborn.
Each new breath of new beginnings
 Showed me the sound
Of vibrations leaving my typewriter
As I pressed the keys.
Abandoning words
My fingers just chased light
As it sparked up
Across the keyboard.

There was a moment
Of time
Where not only did poetry
Flow through me
but, I, myself
Became poetry.

Dad was a poor man
Now he's a rich man

Forgot what it's like to have lungs
                Like hot sand—-
We are sitting on
A grassy field.
It is a spring day.
The grass is taller than
      I remember.

She is here. You know.
THAT girl.
The one from the Chet Baker song.
"Long ago my heart and mind
Got together and designed
The wonderful girl for me."

A giant fish falls
      From the sky—
It almost hits her—-
Why would someone try
To rob me of my longing?

Dad was a poor man
Now he's a rich man
Forgot what it's like to have lungs
                Like hot sand—-

I squeezed my love
      As tight as I could.
The wind was slamming
The tarp against the sheet metal.
Thunder. Eruption. Eruption. Thunder.
Flashes of pale lightening.

I began to pray.
My devotion only arose out of desperation.
Fear had gotten the best of me
I had nothing left.

Whoever the fuck is listening
Get us off this mountain
And I'll do whatever you want!

Something bloomed in me
A message hidden in tremors.
Be my slave?

Willingly, I said.
With the lips of my heart.
The tongue of my soul.

I wish I had more of a choice.
Voluntary or involuntary?
Either way you are
Being admitted for making
Too much noise
With your voice.

I finally slept
And awoke from
A nightmare of red.

Everyone was watching the view
That had been
Hidden in the storm.
The coffee tastes as
Expansive as what we are seeing.

My girl is feeling better.
She thinks it was my love
That healed her.
I am blanked out—
I am empty—
I am gratitude.

Who did I make a deal
             With?
How could I ever know?

Dad was a poor man
Now he's a rich man
Forgot what it's like to have lungs
             Like hot sand—-

Money for bombs! No money for bums!
Money for bombs! No money for bums!
Money for bombs! No money for bums!

At one point I gave up
On society.
Went to go be in the woods of North Carolina
With my dog
Canned beans and my books.

It rained for four days.
I sat in my tent.
Wearing my poncho
From the volcano.
Listening to the patter of droplets.
Reading Basho; waiting.

When the sky cleared
We walked over to the
Dock on the bay
To watch our first sunset.
"Sunset is my favorite color"
Said the freedom woman with purple hair
And wrinkles.

One time in Utah
A red ant told me,
"Your destiny will meet you
Before you meet it."

As I look out
On the changing horizon
A crane came gliding in.
Grazing it's claw gently
On the surface of the water.
Before landing in some tall grass.

I. Am. A. Child.
Like an infant.
In one of those tiny
Blue-tub-pool things.
My father is in front of me.
His hair has no grey.
No stress either.
Why does he have a mustache?

He drags his finger
In the water
And splashes me.

I am back—
On the dock—
Freedom by my side.
Looking at the crane
As it watches the sunset.

Whatever that is….
The invisible slop of the cosmos.
It fills us and connects us.
I see it everywhere.
It's probably because I'm crazy.

Glowing neon fabric string
And like the bee
Die as I leave you with my
                       Sting.

I go home and
       Swallow my pills—-
Always forgetting my
       Hail Mary's—

To dream of a drifter
And his wife.
She asks, where they're going?
To follow my heart
In search of new life.
Love. Hope. Compassion.
Libertad. Poesia. Soy.

Everything Reminds Me of You

The gate keeps them out
And me in—
The electric billboard
With the shifting screen.
It's raining.
The muck in the grout.
The head is on.
Why are you here?

Begin, again.

    Went to that spot
        To look for your glasses—-
            Don't know what I'd do if I found them.
                It's been over three years
                    Since you lost them.
                        What if they
were cracked
                        Dented and dirty?
                Would you accept them?
            Or would time have gone
        On for too long?
      Not long enough?
        To no prevail.
            The glasses were never going
           To be there.
                I just watched my dirty reflection.

There was an older gent.

He had a metal detector

He was listening to the dirt

Or just beneath the surface.

It's all very unclear to those

Who truly face their fears.

    Looking on the horizon.
    Stoic mountains.
    Zen rivers.
        I was beneath a bridge.
            There was a woman

Leaning on the beam.

It wasn't you.

A car honked it's honk.

    I walked my walk.

She was gone.

My fullness felt incomplete.

    Wintertime blues.
    In this summertime heat.

In The Basement of The Art Gallery

Surrounded by glittering drift woood.
A linen cloth pulling
    In the direction
    Of our curiosity.
Mark my body with
    Your stream of smoke.
I am……………surrounded by withering drift wouuuuu-uld.
Uprooted from the stillness
    Of the mountain.
Cast astray in the
    Timelessness of current movement.
Infinitely lost—---
Perdido amor—--
Longing for approval
    Of those who expect self-hate.
Until—-
The creator yanked me
    Made me shine.
Now I am on display.
    For what others celebrate.
All the while
    Brushstrokes live on
In the basement
    Of my basement.

Ruben is Returning

Hola!
Pase mucho
Que no me ves.
Un abrazo fuerte.
Te quiero.
Mucho (3x)
Pasa la bien.

Diamonds and Rust
(**Written at the Ossining Waterfront on earth day. It was raining, I stared at the prison walls and the mighty Hudson.**)

I wish the game of love
Was one I knew how to play.
But if we are being honest.
The only thing I've ever done
With rules is find ways
To break them—-
Perhaps I am a lover.
I've just grown attached
    To my solitude and sorrow.
Applying the laws of love
    As strategy
    In my chess match with death.
What good is your vulnerability
    When the mirror is shattered?
At some point I started
    To see pain in others.
I was young.
Like really young.
For as long as I can remember young—
Did it begin when we were

In church?
Or that time when I was six
    In the bathroom?
Did it begin when the fire
    Was on and the world
    Was barefoot in the grass?
Or when I was ten
And saw my hurting
    Just outside my window?
The first time I swam in warm water?
My dear friend believing my childhood dreams
    Were prophecies of a great wave?
Or when my memories were young
My perspective naive
Too sensitive to believe what I see.
    When someone I trusted hurt me?
When I was tall enough
    To grab the cookies from
    Above the fridge
    For my younger
    Cousins and siblings?
Or when my innocent perspective
    Was raped by society's
    Reality?

When did the sorrow of others
Become a visceral vision
In the gaze of strangers?

I know when I began to
    To control it.
When I first had that
    Red velvet cupcake.

The cream getting on my chin
Licking my lips with gratitude
    For my experience.
With an insistent longing
        For when I could have
           Her next——---
I was a gluttonous fuck,
But a generous lover.

It was so good
        That I got kinda fat—
My tummy brought me
    Great joy.
So good that
The wind flowed
And was filled
        With sea-through ribbons.

This thing—poetry.
    It was deeply compacted
Compressed and compartmentalized.
Into a thing I'd revisit
        When my whole family dies—-
See I was the heir
    Of great masculinity.
Triumphant warriors of
hardship and adversity.
I was the one who was
    Supposed to take over.
That lonely throne
    Built by insecurities,
Courage, and will.

But this bliss was
Far too radiant
To be suppressed.
A divine sensuality
Unfolded my longing.
It picked up a pen
And began to break
Down the fortress
That the scared child had built.
I was filled.

But this was not the first time
I learned how to manage.
To get by.
To lay low.
Buy my time.
See the pain of others
    I can wear it over my heart
    Like a ragged coat.
Or———————————————————————————————————
————————————————————
I can become numb.
To all of it.
Like I can go
Full living breathing
Absurdist snowman.
A full indifference
To whether reality
Ceases or continues.
So much so
That I become entranced
By a predicament
Of the passing moment.

Is it here?
Or then?
Or about to begin?

Reality in these moments
Looks exactly the same
But I am living in a
Compulsory skinny dip
Deep dive through
A fast-moving river.
My lungs are filled with water!
This vessel is being
Pulled down stream.

Perhaps, I am a lover.
I've just grown attached
To my solitude and my sorrow.

I am just trying to live—
    A beautiful truth
While being dependent on
    What is consistent.

But I am inconsistent.

Us poet's can be such
    Mysterious creatures.
When in reality
We just prefer roof tops
Or basements—-
Being outside
    While reciting verse
        To the sun

The birds
The trees.

Like this one time—
I fell asleep in the grass
It was under the shade
Of an elm tree
In Central Park.
I had just finished writing a poem
For a homeless man in
Exchange for some stories—

Nothing he said made
      Any sense.
It was still fascinating.
He was like a living breathing
      Spontaneity.
I had never seen someone
         So broken.
I had never seen someone
         So happy.

My thoughts became
Twisted like a vine.
I needed to rest
And whenever I did
The tree is what I would seek.
It's roots would find me.
Use my typewriter case
As a pillow
With a wallet full
Of cash from
Writing poems.

I dozed off
Under the warm blanket
Of freedom.

And in my dreams
    I was laying naked
    Upon the firmament
    Of a buoyant body of water.
    No land in sight.
    There was a moon in
    That linen evening sky.
    I understood as I looked at it—-
    The real me was
    Over there.
When I awoke
    At the tree across from me
    Was a woman feeding
    Her beagle a peeled apple.

Me, the poet, is not
The judge nor the jury.
We are silent observers

Awaken the dead from the silence
Of their forgotten pulse.

To reveal a truth
To the hidden film
Playing in your head.
The still quilt
Kaleidoscopes through time.
In the speed of the highway

It can slip into our blind spot.

So, if I have to choose—
Love or numb?
Love is my choice.
Making everything I engage with
The citrus of my imagination.

Who am I to say
The homeless broken buddha
Isn't as real as my dream?
Or that my dream isn't
As real as the apple
That the dog ate?

Perhaps—I am a
Naked footed nothingness
Feeling everything run
Through my toes.

I am a lover!
Who has grown attached
    To their solitude and sorrow.
Applying the expression
    Of my love
To take control
In my chess match
    With death!

Happy Birthday!
Happy Birthday!
Happy Birthday!

I Need To Know You Now

Have you ever been to France?
No. I am a desolate man.
I might not know you later,
A deaf song trance.

East river sunrise; a yearning kiss—
Trapped in my memory's imagination.
Remembrance of nothing is bliss.

Gibberish

There is an ant in my room
I grab it's little leg—
I hope to see you soon.
In words no tongue
      Could utter.
Stepped out into glorious views.
A heartbeat truce
Between unrelenting love and pain.
The symphonies inside me
Could drive anyone
      Insane.
When I want to
Express all this hurt
With words of love.
  Covet of my consuming covenant.
I find places that lack your sinking tender.
  This speech will know no stutter.

Only hear; could passion be uttered.

Here come the rapids;
        I HAVE BROKEN THE RUDDER!

The ant squems and resists
I forgive the ignorance
In it's contorts
        And twists.

When things are perilous
It's natural to resist
When life hands
Itself to you
On a paper dish.

Find me at the
        End of the road.
Always cold
Only looks like snow—-
Park benches
        Where my heart unfolds
If this pen was time
Would the story be retold?
In a new light
Where instead of gloves
It was your phantom hand
I hold.

The two anthologies
Of my personality
Are tales of resistance.
Those toward love—

Those toward despair—
It's an attempt
To recover and repair.

I place the ant
In the grass.
To see if it will show me
      A recovered past.
Where all the stories
      To all these
Immaculate scars?

I Am The Grim Reaper

An old person
Has died at the nursing home.
I have been hired
To collect their things.

A man plays Sinatra
On the piano
His fingers remember the melody
His lips have forgotten
      The words.
I am cutting through
His atmosphere.
Carrying boxes and furniture.
None of the wheel chairs
See me.
They only see
A walking hearse.

Lamento Desperado

These fists will only
    Last a moment.
So I've decided to fight
    With my heart.

Soy un hermano
    De la libertad—
Con eso lo digo
    Cuando se que voy a perder—Alli.
Encuentro una luz
    Abajo de la puerta.
Soy un valde de agua.
Un valde de sangre.
Arriba la escalera
Hay umo y tierra.

Soy un hermano
    De la libertad
Un primo del viento.
Escucha el amor
En lo que respiro
Existen dos mundos—-
La guirra spiritual
Estamos perdiendo.

Soy un hermano
De la libertad—-
Un primo del viento—-
Casado con el fuego
Que me quema adentro.

Hay besos calientes
En las lagrimas del cielo.

Olvidate del manana
Tenemos que luchar
Por el momento—-
Por la lucha!
Que tengo que hacer
Si estudes pueden aprender.
Soy uno con la lucha.

Arriba! Y adelante!
Lo que esta pasando
Es un digracia impresionante.

Soy un hermano de la libertad—
Un primo del viento—
Escucha el amor
En lo que respiro—-
Estoy casado con el fuego
Que me quema adentro.

Pero pasen mucho
Y estoy cansado.

Los hijos de la luz
Los estan buscando.
El bosque grita—-
La arena se seca—-
Las montanas estan temblando.

Soy solo un hombre
Que mira

Por sus ojos.
Arriba! Y adelante!
El dinero y el progreso
Estan matando a la gente
Como si fueran piojos.

Arriba! Y Adelante!
La historia del manana
Esta escrita ahora en sus manos.

Amor! Amor! Amor!
Somos familia
Si estamos abajo
Del sol.

Holy Genocide! Holy rape! Holy death! Holy robbery! Holy hunger! Holy theft! Holy waking! Holy rising! Holy rest! Holy starving! Holy murder! Holy carvings! Holy are those trying their best! Holy grass! Holy river! Holy fence! Holy trees! Holy breeze! Holy fire! Holy want! Holy need! Holy forward! Holy still! Holy beat! Holy retreat! Holy are the miles we have walked! Holy are the cuts on our feet!

The Death of a Deer

This is the legend
Of a man
Who for the month
Of May calls himself
    Esperanza.

He wished he

Didn't need her
But when the flowers
    Bloomed it was
    Impossible to not
        Be her.

Are these words ideas
    Or are the ideas words?
Have you heard what I have Heard
when the words
Begin to purr—
The reigns tighten as
The white motorcycle
Pulls away with the ego
Of your hearse.
I bore witness
Instead of a mercy killing—
The truth will tear you
    To pieces,
But then the color
    Of your past
        Will confetti from
        The ceiling—-

It laid itself to rest
Before I can even grieve
The breath—
The spirit of the forest
Was exalted from it's
    Breast.

We are just getting by.

A Prayer To The Moon

Luna llena besame con
        Tu luz.

She only knows pain—
A hairy head; a heart so bald.
Midnight pathway.

Cabernet flows through her veins.
Flames of dry ice can scald.
Tortured by past days.

A stride like tall grass crane—
Her eyes kiss; time will pause.

Luna llena besame con
        Tu luz.

Relieve this bleeding reach;
Staining flowers with lack of hugs.
Grant me remedies to teach
All the way I lack love.

Dark on this journey,
But your light comes from the sun.

Luna llena besame con
        Tu luz.

Allow these healing hands
To mend this broken heart

A not so silent toad
Allow these healing hands;
Let the unfolding to start.
Currents against stones.

Allow these healing hands
To turn trauma into art.
It's starting to feel like home.

Luna llena besame con
          Tu luz.

Reflection was fractured
Your kiss has made it dim.
Now I see a pasture
Listen and movement;
                We begin.

Luna llena gracias por tu beso.
Mi alma esta abrazada
Tengo dolo pero dejo
     En el pasado.

A Cardinal

Eye. Am. The. Red. Cardinal.
Visiting you from the other side.
The embodiment of death.
The protector of life.
Visiting you on branches.
On your typewriter.
In your moments of doubt.

When every direction feels wrong.
The path of my flight goes right.
When every direction is
                Filled with hate.
My wings flutter toward light.

Eye. Am. The. Red. Cardinal.
Hear my songs.
See my stance.
Watch as I fly with deer.
As they roam. Wander. Prance.

Eye. Am. The. Red. Cardinal.
A fifth grader ties a noose.
Eye. Am. The. Red. Cardinal.
A fourteen year old dances with vertigo.
Eye. Am. The. Red. Cardinal.
At eighteen they drag knives
    In their wrist.
Eye. Am. The. Red. Cardinal.
Desolation. They know the taste
        Of iron upon their lips.
Eye. Am. The. Red. Cardinal.
Press that sword to their stomach.
Whirl into the moment of destruction.
Good-bye to the man.
Hello to the bird.
Good-bye to the well.
Hello to the world.
Good-bye knowing land.
Hello ignorant girl.
  (AN: I frequently refer to my own femininity as an ignorant girl.)

Eye. Am. The. Red. Cardinal.
Visiting you from the other side.
The embodiment of death.
The protector of life.
Visiting you on branches.
On your typewriter.
In your dreams.
There I am.
Arriving right in time.
Every direction feels wrong.
In an instance of doubt.
The clouds are gray and long.
Stopped watching the news.
In search of where death belongs,
Listen to the wind.

Eye. Am. The. Red. Cardinal.
How many times have I died?
Just to revisit
      The revision of me
That remains alive.

Eye. Am. The. Red. Cardinal.
Death is my song,
But this soul only flies.

Eye. Am. The. Red. Cardinal.

Remember the forgotten
      There is truth in my gong.

Eye. Am. The. Red. Cardinal.
A messenger from the

Other side.

I see destruction from my trees
      We've aligned with wants
          Instead of needs.
You see a man with a pen
      But he is abandoned breeze.

Smith & Corona Forever

Fear me knot
I load the paper
Pick my plot
An instance savor.

Execute your task—
Execute your past—
The mind is slow.
The finger's are fast.

Not knowing where
      I'll go.
Just ask the whisper
      For a favor.

What can I know?
Abandon the self
      To a flow.
Who he was upon
      The shelf.

The meal is abundant

But he does not
>	Loosen his belt.

Slamming. Clacking.
Sunblaze. Sunset.
An emptying on the page.
Everything is felt.

What does one do?
With all this loving rage.
Some see a gift,
But it can be a plague.

A plague. A plague. A plague.
A soul protected—-
Surrounded by hate.

The bongo poem bangs—
And asses begin to shake.

Children laugh.
People cry.
Beauty within themselves.
They see it in my eyes.
Little do they know
This giver of life—-
Only knows to die.

On a park bench
People passing by—
He watches as they
Carry clock-pulses of time.

Could this be your fate?
Frozen autumn descending leaves.
This machine kills hate.
A mirror of ice;
See me and you will freeze.
A poet-lover playing the field.
Death will be his date—
Wounded in spirit;
He has forgotten his typewriter shield.

An Incognito Bodhisattva

Crimson glory
Endless pastures
Of your infinite home.
Plucked into sound
From silence's time.

Watered by a broken
valve fire house.
Mend your cracked vase
With liquid gold lips.

Royal poinciana;
Hide in your shade,
But the truth
Is in the light.
Neck pricked by grass
Of blade.
Sun kissed cheeks
Your love absolves me
Of my past.

Forest star moss—
You consume lions of
Pride and stone.
Strip you of the dead;
I lay with those who roam
just dream upon your
Decaying bed.

Rambutan, passionate one,
Lychee, Guava, Dragon Fruit,
Apricot, Plum, Watermelon,
Nostalgic Nectarine!!!

I long for a sight so sweet.
A sight so serine.
Yet I only know
       All I've unknown.
Yet to sit with my flavors
       Undone and unsung.
Only to breathe
       What is forgotten
       In hope of benign savor.

A poet-day laborer
       Slams his sledgehammer
Against paper.

By the time they are gone
       The wall is broken
       And they must thank someone,
       For Nirvana's favor.

Expansion and collapse.
Do you hear the humming
Of the reborn universe
      Dying past?
The patterns of time
      Are moving fast.

False Profit #1

Digging for gold
      Fracking the caves
With fluid
Of this tired soul.

Feeling younger than yesterday;
      My body growing old.

How do people turn to you
      When you can barely
      Get out of bed?

All the texts
Left on read.

People speak to me about
Jesus bleeding through the floorboards.
Socrates's poison in my cup.
Zoraster's cave is my agoraphobia.
Rumi's rhythm in the song.

Mujica, Garvey, Muhammed,
Mandela's mandala.

Gandhi, Davis, Lorde,
Lamenting longing
Desperate for more.

They wanna fighter
    I need to play.
Ideas travel faster
    Than words
I say,
I say,
I say,
Fear has me standing for others.
Does that make me a coward
Or brave?
The world is dying,
But it is the mirror
We need to save.
A rambling poet—-absolution is what they crave.

Actions the wood.
Breath the nails.
Standing upon a stage
Of debri
    Burn and crash.
Is it the victor who is standing last?
Intentions are good—
Lead along my path;
    The moments are rash.
Others are profiting off
    My work
While I am short for cash.

False Profit #2

Cortar la lengua
Of your heart
Del corazon
Cut your tongue

To speak with your mouth
Vibraciones de la alma
Vibrations of the soul
Hablar con su boca.

Hablame de flores—
Of sentiment in which noone sees.
Speak to me of flowers.
De sentido que nadie se ven—

Find the barriers of words
El communicacion completa
Then show me with your body
Mostrame con su cuerpo
The language of the whole
Los limites de palabras.

Let your hair down

Do you fear touch?
Lick your lips with my love.
Grip in your clutch—
Down on me; from above.

Fill me with your throb.
Ecstasy. Mercury. Lucid.
Fast ball; What is a lob?
Twist guts in the rhythm
               Of---
Show me your music.

An archer out of practice.
       A misfiring cupid—

A love so deep
The hurt feels stupid.

Shower you with my forgiving stab
Lick your lips; my beloved Judas.

Dim the lights;
good man turned bad.
Comforter stains;
the scent of your pleasure.

Command the madness
Nestle your desire for flight.

A tongue unlocks your treasure.
Poetry spoken into your oozing home.
Thrusts in your eyes.
Observer. Server. Nurture. Learner.

Ascension to the peak
That path of pain
Is lost in love.
Witness to your beauty

Now show me the freak.

Many are the doves
      That cut through rain.
Many are the rain
      That moisten the doves.

False Profit #3

He has been plagued
      By early on set republicanism.
Don't offend me—
Don't tread on me—

Cry baby's cry,
From different branches
On the same burning tree.

White savior complex
Preaching community
      With tyrannical exclusivity
      Ideological captivity.

Projecting offense
Fear of losing or not having
A lifestyle celebrated by all.
Life. Liberty. Prosperity.
A recipe of freedom.
No justice. No peace.
For all. One. All.

Drop the ball

Love is down the hall.
Include your neighbor
    Instead of building a wall.

When the clown removes their make-up

The curtains open
Laughter upon the unicycle
Slips and falls laughter
Creates creatures
Of breath and rubber.
Slips and falls laughter.
Get's pied.
Slips and falls laughter.
The curtains close
Lights dim.
Clown man only reveals
His face to him.
Sips on sorrow
With a glass of gin.
The laughter continues
From beyond his despairing sin.
If only they could hear
Behind his smile
His fight for desire
The cries within.

Happy Rebirth Day

Climb the ladder
Of my spine

Each vertebrae contains
A truth.
If you'd like to
Climb with lies.
I understand—
We all express pain
In the only ways we do.
I will forgive; for it is the only
Thing this foolish heart knows how to prove.
I only ask that when you fill
Your cup with the abundance of my love—
That your hand be gentle.
There is no need to
Break the glass.
Just knock and declare
You are here.
I will consume
Your past
And wash away your fear.
Please tell me you
See your reflection in my eyes.
Don't hesitate to
Shed a tear.
Dying many times
Forgetting to resuscitate.
Lonely years normalized.
My compassion is awfully arrogant.

False Profit #4

Mother, I have abandoned you.
You were never mine to hold.

Father, I have abandoned you.
You only knew me from over there.
My brothers I have abandoned you.
The sound of your names
Are tattooed in my heart.
My sisters I have abandoned you
May my lips find your forehead soon.
My children I have abandoned you
Your ancestors abandoned me.
Now inherit the darkness of their caves.
Learn to build fires.
So that even shadows
Are embraced by light.
Carry yourself with the
Beauty of the day.
Carry yourself with the honesty of night.

Untitled

Great grandmother
Pour your wine
From your lilly rose.

Great grandfather
Give me a chisel
And a calloused hand.
So I may carve out the stone of a better man.

Ballad Of A Civil Rights Alchemist

Hello, Ms. Hollywood Highway----
Mr.Rebel without a cause---

Zombies until Friday.
The fight has no pause.

You see it your way----
Your words are your laws---

I see it my way.
Silent destruction in the halls.

Drag your knife in my skin.
Behead my child---
Here comes the ram.
Where do we begin,
elected Son Of Sam?
Soul is strong, but growing thin
The pleasures of the damned.
Turn my compass dial---
Watch, as the critics become fans.

A false profit sings a hymn---
A false profit sings a hymn---
A false profit sings a hymn;
let them in.

{Chorus}
What will tomorrow bring?
Will you linger
Or help me sing?
Freedom is dying

The algorithm's lying.
The poet-child lays crying
while our mother's soil;
she lays frying.

The nexus of exodus
Napalms names.

Grace upon hell's precipice?
Is God's madness to blame?
No, solution just messages.
The fires of love are generous .
Tired eyes witness pain.
Could this love be misgauged?

These words are venomous
I will poison you with love.
Take the stone from Sisyphus
All he needs is a hug.

The hurting cop; a gun to point.
Detectives cry over common hurt.
A whirling mechanic anoints.
Bury your secrets in the dirt.

{Chorus}
What will tomorrow bring?
Will you linger
Or help me sing?

Freedom is one.
    Together for disdain.
Alone we are none.

Penetrate meme membrane.

Give me color or give me death!
The road; you walk alone.
Is there whiskey on your breath?
How lonely is your throne?
Get the words off your chest;
a dog without a bone.

We are trying our best;
Us river sinking stones.

Momma, why'd you plant me
Away from marigolds?
Humming with honey bees
A truth I've been told.
Growing into me;
your sundews have been sold.

A piece of what you make
The hours are growing old.
A piece of what your make
the hours are growing old.
A piece of what you make;
away from marigolds.
A piece of what you make;
a truth I've been told.

What will tomorrow bring?
Will you linger
or help me sing?

Ms.Hollywood Highway---
Mr.Rebel without a cause---
Dance. Here. Today.
Love brings problems
from the law---
Living in my monitor---
Don't want to see
what I saw---
So. They monitor.
The way this soul makes
people pause---

What will tomorrow bring?
Will you linger
or help me sing?

Free the prisoner
living in your mind.
Free the prisoner
victim of the times.

Eat the rich
they are guilty of war crimes.

False Profit: In dedication to the chosen river #5

Sink or swim?
This movement
Can't tell when
There is water

On all sides.
High on heresy.
Proclaiming passion
Reluctant with love.

Sink or Swim?
If we surrender
Could we walk on water.
Will never—
Too distracted by the waves.

Recovering the souls of others.
Will mine ever be saved?

My trumpet is submerged
Can you hear the last song in the descending bubbles of air?

Swimming to the bottom
Grass creaking
On yesterday's song
Silence is the expectation.
Education turns
Into fascination.
Learn to listen
The world is vast.
But you are expanding.
Pay attention…

You are a—
Premonition.
Of this long forgotten sea.
A whale battles a squid—-
I watch in the relic garden of me.

The Girl in Guatemala

I am sorry—
You found me in
Broke windows.
I left you on the pier.
There was a man fishing
In the distance.
I fished my pockets
Hoping a ring would appear.

I'm sorry—-
You found me in the north.
I left you in the warm humid south.

I am sorry—
You found me with your love.
I left you with my hurt—

I am sorry—
You found me with
Your kiss.
I left you with my words.

I am sorry—
You found me with your life.
I left you with my death.

I am sorry
You found me with your nourishment
I embraced you in my desperation.

Was any of it real?

I am sorry---
That despite the efforts
You chose steal
Instead of too feel.

An Agnostic Prayer

To whom it may concern,
I am trying my best.
So, when I die
Don't let it burn.

To whom it may concern,
I surrender to your guidance,
But I must admit
It is difficult for me to learn.

To whom it may concern,
Grant me strength.
If you are willing and
Don't forget patience too.

I have witnessed your beauty
I'd like to believe
But I've seen your
Suffering too.

To whom it may concern,
Show me the path

To forgive the ways
I have been forced to burn and crash.

To whom it may concern,
I'd like a new future
Not a repeat of my past.

False Profit #6

I identify as a heretic
One hurting and humiliated.
But this must be better than your messiah memes.
Living in your pocket
Prescribing what you need
When the selfies are away
It is only misery.

I fear power.
I don't do well with attention.
Lied to too much.
Forgotten how to trust.
Jesus bleeds through the walls
To let me know my divine suffering
Is just testicular retention—
If only I could be touched...
Instead I touch myself
To the idea of every gasp
I once knew.

I am dependent on dependency
Nothing validates me like a glass of whiskey
You see me drinking alone
But I hear the meter

Of my poetic ancestors
In the clinking of glass on ice.

Suddenly I am not alone
And I have drowned the sorrows
Of my past.---
Temporarily.

The pills make me feel like
A wool sweater—-
I struggle to take them.
The only thing I am good at
Is being honest.
If we are being honest
About the world
Wouldn't you be a little manic?

And despite all the mayhem
My message is don't panic.
There can be no mischief in the shadows
If the light of love
Shines bright.

So, demand the change you want to see
Through an unruly love of life!

I identify as a heretic.
Their lies will be consistent.
And my truth is filled with contradictions.

Look into the eyes of strangers
Find lovers with conviction.
Plan for a new world

Push the ones you love—

In the direction of something different

An Ode to Building Bridges

I am. You are.
Neither one of us are engineers.
But maybe we can figure it out.

My guess...
Is it will take laborers.
My guess...
Is it will take more than what we are doing.

You are. I am.
Together we must persevere.

My guess...
Is it will take more than one.
My guess...
Is the water will run.
Some possessions might slip through our fingers.
Our watch is too loose
As we lay the foundations
And get caught in the current.

She is him. They are her. He is she.
An intimate difference is what we fear?

The weather in the north east require
Flexibility---bend---sway.
The weather to the west
Requires embrace
for the tremors
Of shifting plates.
The south is humid.
We need material that is—
Willing to expand and understand.

We are. We are. We are.
Not engineers.
But the resources on this side aren't used up.
We need to get to the other side.
Come together see eye to eye.
Seeing violence in the world; seeing violence in our mind.
Take our time—-begin to unwind.

It will take time to rebuild
The way the old bridge was built.
To unrape.
To unmurder.
To unplague.
To unallienate.
To ungenocide.
The way we process indifferent indifference differently defensive.

If we are going to die,
I'd like to say I tried.
Bridges between division,
 Are really bridges to the sky.

Part Two

Meditations

7

Nowhere Man

The parts that are underlined are me presently commentating on a piece of writing from when I was in college. This essay was an essay I wrote as my senior thesis. My professors helped me work towards a final project that supported the studies I did while also helping untangle the mess my life had become. They were aware of the story I went through from word of mouth and what I had told them. They knew that my interests aligned with an idea akin to living an aesthetic life. Though I initially approached them about was writing about the desire to have a perfect death. What I had, after about six months of therapy and self work following the event that turned my life upside down, discerened was the motivation behind a suicide attempt. My professors selected a series of books and articles for me to read. We would read them together and meet once a week to discuss the books theoretically. It was my responsibility to use the work that we read in a way that accomplished the standard criteria of my degree and something far deeper for myself.

The commentary I will be making will be from beyond a certain veil of ignorance I had towards my circumstances. Certain things have come to the surface about the time I am writing about since writing it. Things that somewhat alter the narrative. Ever so slightly. But not insignificantly. I will admit that my approach in editing and making commentary will be to a minimal.

I think there is a certain obligation toward the truth that may force me to interject, but for the most part I want the piece to stand on it's own. Because even if it isn't one hundred percent the truth it was a striving towards one. A striving that had me recognized by the philosophy department when I was awarded upon graduation.

The knots are too tangled. If you are looking for clear cut answer of what my life has been I'll give you an answer that you'd probably give me. "Pretty good. A fair deal of shit storms, but overall not too bad.". More rodeos than I can count, but that comes with being who you are.

I am under the impression that this work might have been published or circulated without my consent. So if this is your first time reading this, coolio mustardman. But if it is not your first time then I hope you can still find a way to engage with the writing and my commentary in a way that is enjoyable.

Here is a very brief story. The events of this story are very much isolated to a specific time frame. But the sequencing of events capture a certain pattern that reoccurs throughout my life. If I were to write an autobiography, then this would be a chapter of the book. A chapter that if I have accumulated any degree of notoriety it would be in this era of my life. At least amidst the unforgiving masses. Admittadly an opinion that used to be very important to me.

NowHere Man

"I cannot paint / what then I was." (1), but I will try my best.

My younger brother inquires, "What is going on?" with genuine fear in his eyes. He should be used to me falling apart, but, I guess, how does anyone get used to seeing their older brother destroy themselves. It's February 2023 we should be in class but we are in North

Carolina, it's raining and it's cold. My brothers have been my best friends since I can remember. I am ready to give it all away. All I have worked for means nothing to me now. I just want the open road and nature. <u>I have been drawn to living a beatnik lifestyle since reading about the adventures of Chris McCanedless. The way my life has played out I don't know if I'll ever be able to life a life of such silent and liberating aninmonity.</u> But they weren't ready to give up on me the way I was ready to give up on myself. Let's rewind a bit.

Size ten and a half timberland boots. Laced all the way to the top. Blue jeans with compound and paint stains. My grey tee shirt also has a mosaic of fingerprints in paint. I grab my coffee and lunch in the morning with callied hands. I find peace in painting walls or framing them or sheet rocking them. Character was built behind a wheel barrel. Wheel barrels filled with cinder blocks or stones or sand or cement or mulch or anything really. I faced my fear of heights when roofing or carrying material up ladders. Fanon has a theory that when you learn a language you reveal new elements of your personality. (2). In my five years of working with immigrant coworkers the spanish language became a refuge for my imagination. I'd drive by cars and create background stories based off their facial expression and the model of their vehicle. Sometimes at Home Depot I'd try to guess someone's favorite sex postion based off the way they walked. This was four years ago. Before college and countless books. Life was simpler back then. A cold beer after working a hot day in the sun was enough to move me to a state of cool bliss. Perhaps, life still is this simple and it is I who have become needlessly complicated. I never intended to be a poet. As Plato says through Socrates, "That by beauty beautiful things become beautiful." (3). Or to reframe it, *That by poetry the poet becomes poetic.*

Come 2019 and construction was no longer my occupation. I was in school and working as a bank teller. I found myself at the bottom of a bottle and half way through a Charles Bukowski novel. I decided to light a candle, turn the lights off, and sit on the floor. I had picked up the habit of meditating via my readings of Allan Watts and Shunryu Suzuki. Maybe fifteen minutes into meditating in this dimly lit room I was hit with a pang of euphoria. I was embraced by the full fluidity of being. A deep understanding of my own pain and pleasure enveloped me. I began to weep. Twenty three years old, far away from home for the first time, and completely alone. I grabbed a notebook and began to write. Writing in rows and calling it poetry with no sense of rhythm, meter, or form. <u>I still don't know what the fuck that shit is.</u> What I did once for the first time in ten years became a habit. I was writing poetry everychance I got.

In May 2020, I moved back home to Westchester and that's when my habit really picked up. I wrote five poems a day for the whole summer. More <u>often then not turning them into one poem that I liked and throwing away the scraps.</u> My philosophies were from scratch and not half bad. When I began to show my friends what I was writing there was a shift in my style.

I began to write with this in mind: For every existence there is a narrative; that narrative is either beautiful or tragic based on your perspective. This was my guiding principle for two years of my life and it blossomed from the belief that empathy is the highest good. It lead to two years of spontaneity. Two years of magic. Two years of poetry.

I spent the rest of 2020 studying, writing, and falling in love. I did the same for most of 2021. In the summer of 2021 myself and "The Highwaymen" raced across the country in a silver dodge mini van. We did New York to California continuously. The only time we stopped was to camp in Moab. We slept under the stars, let the clay absorb us and in the morning we were reborn in the crisp air. After feeling the freedom of the open road I knew one thing, I didn't want to work a normal job again. I needed to be a writer. My hobby metamorphosized on the long straights of blacktop into a profound vocation.

From October 2021 to October 2022 I'd strap a twenty five pound bag to my back and take the journey into New York City towards Central Park. Three times a week for a year. In that bag was a nineteen eighties Smith and Corona type writer (she is baby blue and gentle), a few notebooks, my current journal, and some piece of literature. I'd carry a television table and a sign that read, "Pick a topic–get a poem.". I lived as beat poet. <u>A Charlie Brown Beat. I was a committed to my relationship, but looked at the world and everybody with a sympathetic glossy eye.</u> I grew my hair long and began conjuring up fables about squirrel kings or girls trip to new york or love or loneliness or loss. And plenty of others. But like all things it came to an end. I am interested in the poet's place in the world. What responsibility does the poet have? Toward themselves and towards the potential that is awakened through action? For action, or art and poetry, is the place where potential transforms into quality or value. Could art instead be the interpretation of the imagination?

My first day out there was extraordinary. It begins like this, a friend of mine, Figo, went to Colorado and got a poem from a stranger. When he came back from his trip he gifted it to me and showed me the video of the poet typing away on his typewriter. This was a Friday.

COVID had happened to everyone in so many different ways. What it did for me was slow the pace of my world to the point where I found poetry again. I wrote my first poem when I was in the eighth grade and aside for the occasional english project, I had walked away from writing as a whole. The isolation and the retreat caused by the pandemic allowed me to rediscover poetry. I was unemployed, drinking tea, and walking barefoot in the grass. I was directionless, but privileged and perhaps this is why I was able to write so prolifically. I had adopted the principle of, "First thought, best thought." long before I had become in the writings of Kerouac and Ginseberg. I was showing my closest friends the flowers I was tucking away in my poetry notebook.

Despite all their praise I never considered myself a poet, rather poetry is something I could do. Not something I am. Or will become. My ambitions in writing was/is to be a novelist. Either way poetry is, like all art, a conduit of change. I am reminded of the final line from the poem by Rilke. After describing a statue that depicts the beautiful torso of Apollo he abruptly declares, "You must change your life." (4). As this final line of this poem depicts poetry is the cause of something. What that something is can be elusive, but we know that it creates change in the audience.

Anyways, it was a Friday that I was shown the poem from Colorado and we agreed to meet at the train station on Sunday. Him and his girlfriend would bring a sign. My girlfriend at the time and myself would bring the poetry. My older brother had gifted me a typewriter for Christmas and I spent all day Saturday slamming away. I had a dictionary that I would flip to a random page and ask a family member what the first word they saw was. I would then run to my room and write a poem about that word. On the eve of my first day out there I wrote about twenty poems.

One thing to be noted about writing is that it is more of a rhythm than a discipline. The discipline isn't in the act but in the consistency of the act. That made no sense. <u>It still doesn't.</u>

So the first day happens. I take the train to the city with these three close friends. We stop at Bryant Park and it's no good. I feel too much of the city atmosphere. I am in need of nature. I suggest Central Park. We make our way over taking turns carrying my typewriter, which isn't in its bag (It would take a couple of weeks before I bought a backpack big enough to carry it) but inside a metal briefcase. When we finally arrived, I sat down before the women's rights statue, Figo took a phone call, Anna Leah took my photo, and then they left. It was just me, a cool October day, a park bench, and my typewriter. They were only a shout away, but I felt the immense weight of my new endevor. Depending on how today goes I might not ever have to get a regular job again. Maybe I can do this forever and just live this life? To live as a busker in NYC. The freedom of this lifestyle enticed me.

The first couple approached. They asked for a poem about a timeless moment. How easy!? Poetry is precisely that. Timeless moments captured on the page. So, I wrote completely present. To nature, to the presences before me, to time. I moved as fast as I could and before a thought registered I was at the bottom of the page. The timeless moment had run out of time. So I pulled it from my typewriter quickly glanced at the words that hadn't fully registered in my mind and handed it over. A piece of myself gone just like that. The girl began to tear up and the man handed me a twenty as he repeatedly told me how talented I was. Twenty dollars in five minutes! For writing! I am a paid writer! How could I ever go back a nine to five? I was no longer Dario, I was Ruben De Escapado. A fantasy I had adopted by being a disrupter to others. I signed each poem with this pen name. *Ruben The Escaped.* <u>The question dawns on me that I have no idea what I escaped. Or what I was trying to escape. The name came to me in a time that I will mention in the next essay</u> *The Art of Loneliness.* <u>A dark period of my life filled with solitude and resentment. The name came somewhat naturally.</u>

Something more remarkable happened that day that still puzzles me. When I handed the poem over the eyes of the recipients would illuminate. I could never make sense of it.

In Plato's Ion, Ion a rhapsode has just returned from winning a poetry competition. Socrates questions Ion about the nature of poetry. Socrates backs Ion into a corner, does the rhapsode who specializes in one artist (in this instance Ion was a master rhapsode of Homer's poetry and Homer alone) know nothing or is he divinely inspired? Ion chooses the latter. The conclusion of the argument is that the poet is divinely inspired and that the rhapsode is next on the link of inspiration. Imagine divine inspiration to be a magnet, to paraphrase Plato, and the poet is the first iron link. The next link is the rhapsode. The final link the audience. That through poetry and the reciting of poetry the inspiration is transferred via a link. Perhaps that link is quality, or potential becoming quality.

Now I do not consider myself to be divinely inspired. I am even a sketpic towards the nature of spontaneity. But I do think that performance art like I was doing is cause to awe. The speed in which the poem is written alongside the power of poetry leads to shock in one major way. The recipient of the poem hears the clacking of my typewriter and sees me in a deep state of concentration. They begin to develop ideas of their own. In other words they write a poem in their head while I write one on the page. A poem filled with anticipation. Then when I hand it over, it's inevitably different from their expectations. Through this dismantling of expectations the recipient is left in a state of disruption, which wipes them clean for a moment. A guiding principle of Zen Buddhism is a beginners mind. "In the beginners mind there are many possibilities; in the masters there are few." (5). I believe through poetry on demand I opened the reader up to the possibilities. This feels like a more realistic explanation than divine inspiration in my case, but perhaps they are the same thing. I don't have an answer to this phenomenon, but what I can offer is my experience. In the year that I busked, I'd always watch the eyes of the recipient as they scanned the page. Then the final line and boom, there was a glimmer that wasn't there before the poem. Or when writing poems of grief, sadness, or loneliness the eyes would well up. Poetry provides perspective and solace more than anything. "That is the beauty of literature. You discover that your longings are universal longings, that you're not lonely and isolated from anyone. You belong." (6). Perhaps this is what was identified as divine inspiration. That poetry is the avenue for us to return to our humanity. A humanity that contains passion and sorrow simultaneously. When we reconnect with these universal longings we inevitably reconnect with ourselves in a deeply intimate way.

Why me? <u>Like why did anyone bother to take a chance?</u> My position on that park bench displayed that I was on the margins of society.

I had not become one of the many who lose themself to the mundane. If we take divine inspiration to be a literary tool as opposed to an actual thing, then my role as a writer was to awaken them to the divinity they contained within themselves. People kept coming to me because they saw my position in the world and assumed I knew something they didn't. They saw divinity within me and I saw it in them. In the Symposium, Socrates shows up late because he was arguing with a demon. Despite his apparent madness Alcibades wants to sit near Socrates. For Socrates has knowledge of the truth and he wants it to rub off on him. This is what it was like sitting on that park bench. Because I was outside the mundane, I contained an eccentricity that enticed others, but was also my demise. I too have argued with demons.

On that first day out there I wanted to dance and sing. Later in my journey as a busker I would dance and sing. But today this immense ecstasy was retrained. If art is the interpretation of the imagination then it is also the exploration of the imagination. Through this exploration we reveal elements of our psychology with each line. This is, in many ways, the path toward actualization. But the imagination is a powerful thing and should be explored with caution. One thing you should know about me as I continue on my exploration is that I lost my mind to poetry. Thoroughly lost it.

That first day I made close to three hundred dollars. I rode the train that afternoon with a great conviction of identity and self worth. I vowed to live the life of a poet. Not only did I vow to live as a poet but I was to perfect it. <u>What an incredibly foolish mistake!</u> At this point in time I still had no technical understanding of what it meant to write <u>(I still don't!)</u> which is what made my work so original and authentic. The beauty of poetry is it can be conducted in ignorance. I was quite literally making it up as I went. Writing lines on a page and calling it poetry without the slightest idea of what a poem truly consisted of. Just knowing the type of poems I liked and trying to emulate them. This was October and in December I had enough money from busking stashed away to move into an apartment with Anna Leah. I was being paid for my work and getting to enjoy the fruits of my labor.

Why me?

I still had a philosophical duty. See my perspective–one being refined by excessive writing and studying literature and philosophy along with my experiences–was unequivocally unique. Everyone's perspective is unique, but most remain dormant to themselves.

I had met other philosophers and writers and my advantage was my busking. I had met other buskers and my advantage was my studies. No matter what circle I was in, I always contained a wild card of experience. <u>Life has humbly taught me that I am not that unique. It is my lack of uniqueness that in fact makes me special.</u> What was my duty? The only answer I had was to document it all. I journalled religiously. I'd document my day, which for the most part was slow. It wasn't one or two poems every hour, it was more akin to fifteen to twenty poems for an hour then nothing for two hours and then another burst. These down hours is when I would do personal writing or dive through a book. There was only one day where I didn't stop writing. I made nine hundred and eighty dollars by writing close to eighty poems. I know how many I wrote because I ran out of paper and began tearing sheets from the back of my journal. So in those down hours I'd write essays, reflections, or poetry. One question that I revisited a number of times was, what is love? This is the one subject that which I consistently would freeze up. I had a notion of love, I was *in* love with Anna Leah. But to be in love doesn't mean you know what it is. It was always a difficult question but I would ask myself. I didn't think a twin flame was a factual thing, but the best explanation for what real love is like. It's warmth in the winter. I thought it was the best explanation until I read the Symposium by Plato. I took a specific interest in Diotima's ladder but we will talk more about that when we get closer to lava.

The physician Eryximachus elaborates from the perspective of a naturalist stating that there exists a harmonizing and all-pervasive influence of love in all things. I felt this when I went to the park and connected with strangers. I believe in some way we all contain a spirit or a soul. A cosmic force that we are granted at birth and return with death. A sort of intangible substance that fills our physical experience with perspective and opinion. Perhaps we are always dying, and when we forget that fact we are not in reality but in fantasy. Anyways, this cosmic force interacts with other forces, just by being in the general facinity, and we can become very sensitive to these interactions. To become sensitive to these interactions could be viewed as the meaning of art. Do I dare, the meaning of life? By immersing ourselves in the arts (When I was in construction I felt this same refinement occurring when learning a new skill) we expand our consciousness and refine our intuition.

Then, in the Symposium, Aristophones, the comic poet, discusses the origin of sexes. Stating that we were once a single being and with time have divided. Love is the imperfect being finding their other part. This is what I felt towards Anna Leah. We had touched eachother the way a skipping rock encounters the air and the water at once. Leaving greater ripples behind until we finally made it work. We sunk to the bottom of the lake and looked up at fish flying over head. When it worked it was the greatest pleasure I have ever known. We rediscovered our youths in one another. Even when we fell apart it wasn't bad. It was just the friction of growth in different directions coming to the surface. She was my biggest supporter. I couldn't have gone out there every weekend if it wasn't for her. So when we fell apart it only makes sense that this was around the time I stopped busking in Central Park.

Let's recap. I start going to Central Park. I make enough money to move out. I'm living with Anna Leah in the Bronx. The winter hits. It's January so I have off from school and I decide to throw myself at writing. Harder than I have ever gone before. I write everyday in my novel, (working title) One More Cup of Coffee <u>now that I understand how the self-publishing process works I am finally going to publish</u>

it!, and came up with four chapters in the month. I did this by writing for eight hour days for four days a week. Monday through Thursday. Then on Fridays and Saturdays going to the city. At night I'd drive for DoorDash to make up the difference from tourism being down. Sometimes I was going out there and only doing one or two poems. But I was obsessed with the craft of busking and more than anything I believed in it.

When my spring semester rolls around my terabyte dies on me and I lose the four new chapters. Alongside my short stories, a summer's worth of poems, and college career's worth of writing. I felt it was my ambition testing me; the next day I opened the word document and proceeded onward. I had the chapters back by the end of March. As it warmed up more people began to pour in. I was reminding myself each day that I hadn't lost "it". I was basking in my independence and living poetically. Girls and guys would make eyes at me just so my ego would inflate. There was this chinese man who would exquisitely play classical music on the Erhu and then happy birthday. There was this guy who wore slippers and would play the steal drum. There were my fellow buskers who were cranking out poetry down the way. There was a painter off her medication. A saxophone player with a bass voice. My friend the guitar man, who had a mustache and played music in Germany. There were college students convinced that consciousness was shared and through synchronicity we all become one. There was an Opera singer from Los Angeles living in Brooklyn. He rode a bike and was fascinated by Einstein's theory of relativity. We may or may not have consumed illicit substances together. That day I believed in divine inspiration in it's most romantic way. The keys on my keyboard illuminating like whack-a-mole as I chased them with my fingers. Seeing the sound ripple out the sides.

There was Tom an engineer who was obsessed with Mark Twain. He told me that the one thing that makes a man a man is that they show up. He wanted a poem for his wife. A love poem. When he read it he declared that I knew love and laid a fat kiss on me. A fat sweaty kiss. I wrote a poem about the color blue for a japanese girl named Blue. I went to the women's rights march then the following day listened to Pitbull talk about politics on the stage behind me. I fell in love with a french girl for a conversation. I fell in love with a belgian painter for a conversation. There was always live music. The birds were chirping. The squirrels were friendly. People were always in a good mood. I was always in a good mood. It was when I'd ride the six train home that I would recognize the way my vocation was disarming me. The alienation of the dystopia that is New York.

My first major encounter with psychosis <u>I was trying to write in a way that was validating for therapists and family members. Who are attemtping to understand what I had gone through. Whether this event was psychosis or not two things are abundantly clear. I am not an individual prone to psychosis though a stressed enduced event may have occurred. If it was internal or external phenomenon I will never know. What I do know is what I went through was one of the most miraculous moments of my life. I hope one day I can write about this event in more detail.</u> occurred around the end of that spring. I had written about forty poems–It was a busy friday. I had made good cash and Anna Leah wanted to go to the botanical gardens the next day. I have a long history with suicidal ideation and there is usually an increase with fatigue. This woman messages me as I am going to bed. I have no intention of going but she says that she is from Colorado and that she wanted to see me. I asked Anna Leah if we could go Sunday to the botanical gardens and she said it wasn't a problem; she would replant her plants. So I went.

I gave a five to one of the street performers as I walked by; a superstition for good karma. Make my way to the park bench and set up shop. At this time I was bringing an extra notebook and asking people for a creative exchange. While I wrote them a poem, you take a page and do as you please. I always recommended a drawing, a trick I picked up from the french girl I fell in love with. My body and my heart always belonged to Anna Leah. These moments of love were like flutters. Wind against chimes.

I breezed out the first poem. A good sign for the day. Writing was either like chewing rocks or roller blading on smooth pavement. Today seemed to be smooth pavement, despite my fatigue which meant more suicidal ideation then normal. I wish in those moments I could think about the people I loved but all I want is to be not where I am. Then the second woman approaches. She is the one who messaged me the night before. She is disheveled. Her hair is a mess, her shirt is stained, her pants are the same, she is wearing sandals and socks, and her yorki looks like it's been spun in the dryer. She tells me that her brother was her last family and he has killed himself. No warning signs. He just did it. She showed me pictures from their childhood and more recent ones as adults. My task was to write a poem. I asked her to draw me a picture. It's a lonely stick figure drawing of a boy and a girl climbing a mountain. She walked away and gave me a chance to think. I started to work on something when two algeriens approached me. One had hoops in his ears. The other had a hoop on his nose. They both wore baggy clothes. "You are like zee Keroauc?" I had just finished reading Tristessa and my admiration was growing by the day. "Yes! I am like Keroauc.". We began talking about the books we were reading. I showed them my copy of Moon Palace by Paul Auster. They showed me a copy of The Rebel by Camus. I told them I was a fan of Camus. They told me to read Joseph Kessel. And then I moved them along because "I am writing a poem about suicide.". "Ahhh you are zee fan of Camus.". What I came up with was sub par. But I handed it over either way. I was too distracted. This woman, how she looks, that would be my family if I ever acted on the thoughts I was having. Turns out I was chewing rocks. She leaves and a lesbian with her gay friend approach me, that is how they identified themselves to me. She takes my book and writes a poem for a poem. It reads:

"A Poem For a Poet"

Pouring out of yourself, day after day
Do you ever feel empty?
Or do the words of strangers somehow fill
Your cup?
Wave after wave of emotive expressions
And reaching into the depths of
Your imagination–do you ever
Drudge up something just for you?

At the end of the day, is it an
Overflow or an emptiness that
Carries you into your bed–spent?

Do you feel our gratitude?

    I didn't have a good answer, but after feeling like I failed for the suicide poem and reading this poem, I was wiped. Oscar Wilde in his preface to Dorian Grey says, "The moral life of man forms part of the subject-matter of the artist, but the morality of art consists in the perfect use of an imperfect medium."(7). Wilde believes there is no social function in art. Art just is. To create something in the pursuit of perfection despite the piece being inevitably imperfect was the only moral function of art. It is best performed for one's own sake. Was I considering my social image too much and not caring enough about filling my poetry notebook again? I made maybe $60 and called it quits for the day. I packed up and found a more secluded park bench. I took out the book and a joint. "Vice and virtue are to the artist materials for an art." (7). I sparked it up and looked over the drawings and the poem. What was my responsibility to these people? Wilde would argue that I don't have one to them. Mathew Arnold would say that through my art I must cultivate the elevation of their consciousness. As a creative did I have an obligation to convey specific ideas? To awaken people to themselves. To let them know that we are overstimulated and overcafinated into a hypnosis of ideals and empty progress. A notion of progress that is only concerned with what is next and what is best not what is now and what will stand the test.

I met a woman out there once and in a single conversation she opened my eyes. I hold onto two things she said. The first, "You must ask yourself three questions. One, do these people know the truth? Two, do they deserve to know the truth? Three, do you have the right to tell them?". The second thing she said that stuck is that, "Sometimes compassion looks like a moment of pain for a lifetime of joy.". I carry these words with me everytime I write.

I am smoking my joint and pondering over the sunset. Do I do more? Do I throw myself at activism and use my skills of communication to help others? Do I continue on my mission? At the grass roots, one person at a time awakening them to the power of their own perspective? Do I stop coming out here all together, get a normal job, and write as a hobbyist again? "To be, or not to be / That is the question." (8). Like Hamlet I was left with indecision. The impending night chill of early summer, the echoes of a distant city, my contemplation, and the K2 I was smoking left me in a paranoid state. So in the lingering heat of the day I decided to make my journey home. To return to safety, love, and freshly plotted plants.

I passed the brick arches and beared right at the fork. As I was making my way out of the park there were two young men in striped shirts. One of them offered me a beer. They were taking it out of the case and stuffing it in their bag. Either psychosis or divine inspiration. I have differing opinions based on the day. But I was convinced that the young man offering me the beer was the reincarnation of Jack Kerouac. His friend was Neal Cassidy. I couldn't utter a word. I just accepted the beer and looked back when I crossed the street. They made their way down fifth avenue, arm in arm. I can't make sense of it. Nor do I try anymore.

One day shortly thereafter, we, Anna Leah and I, were house sitting for my parents. We googled "cheap flights". One of the first results was Guatemala. "What to do in Guatemala". The top three results were "1. Antigua Guatemala. 2. Hike Acatanango. 3. Lake Atitlan.". We searched Airbnb for places. Busking was going better and we booked the cheapest flight for July. Or june. I don't remember. Building up to the trip I was having stranger and more deeply personal interactions. The trauma from COVID had effected the world. Every square inch of it. People were coming and I was being their therapist. People will confess if you listen with an open heart. Also, poetry is taught in prison's so that prisoners develop a therapeutic way to express themselves (9) and I was witnessing the therapeutic power of my words.

The day before leaving for Guatemala I go to Central Park. I am having a smooth pavement type of day. I am seated a little further down then I normally do. A woman paces before me. She walks past then turns around and walks past again. She does this about five times until she sits besides me. It's a cool summer day but it's still warm. She is wearing a fleece coat and a skirt. The first thing I notice when she says hello is her teeth and her breath. They have chickled down to nothing and it is putrid. She has stopped brushing months maybe years ago. Two minutes into the conversation it is clear she is completely neurotic. I remind myself that patience is a virtue as she disregards my offer for a poem and begins a conversation about life and madness.

We spoke about the totalitarian family she grew up in. How expectations pushed her too far. How she got laid off by a major financial firm and since she has gotten addicted to caffiene (probably some other things as well). She opened her phone and this seemingly homeless woman had four hundred and fifty thousand dollars in her bank account. I told her to get out of the city for a while. To rent a home in the country and decompress. We ended up talking for almost two hours. The whole time she kept tying and untying an eyecover in her hair as if it were a pony tail. At one point I asked her if she was writing anything down. She said "What do you mean?" and I said "Like a journal.". She responded with "Not like this." and then rolled up her sleeve. From her finger tip to her neck she had written all over herself. On both arms. The only words I could make out were bullet, dent, and helmet. She then showed me a picture of her apartment and the walls were covered in writing. It was a miracle to me that this woman was holding herself together the way she was. That isn't to say she was handling life well but all things considered she could have a conversation. She was able to focus on one thing at a time and was receiving what I was telling her. She told me the caffeine and lack of sleep were giving her out of body experiences. At the end of our conversation we called her old therapist and scheduled an appointment. I then needed to pack up my things and leave otherwise she would have talked endlessly. I wrote her a poem about vanilla ice cream. I write about her because on my trip to Guatemala my understanding of love would radically change. And my journey of love begins by encountering her madness. I saw myself in her. No matter how I try to manuever it madness and love feel deeply intertwined. Love makes us do things that we would never do otherwise. Why else was I about to hike an active volcano? Because I'd be doing it with her, of course.

 Anna Leah and I take off. We arrive in Guatemala City and as soon as we leave the airport a child throws up right in front of Anna Leah. She barely dodges it as we make our way to our car. This was a good omen believe it or not. The cab driver is also a tour guide and is very trust worthy. We tell him we are going to Antigua tomorrow and as he drops us off at the hostel he offers to pick us up. We take him up on it and in the morning he gets us after breakfast. The whole ride over he is telling us about his adventures. His wife is in the passenger seat and is showing us photos of him up different mountains. He offers to take us up Acatanango, but we already paid for an expedition group. He tells us to buy warm clothes at the market and which tequila to bring for the mountainmen.

When we arrived at our Airbnb it was a dream. There was the ruins of an old church before us. There was volcanoes surrounding us. The sun was setting and the clouds were large and soft on the eye.

In Plato's symposium, Socrates explanation of love comes in the form of Diotima's ladder. A ladder with a series of rungs. Each rung means a deeper understanding of love. A deeper definition of the very word. In many ways Diotima's ladder mirrors Pater's view on surrounding yourself with art. The more we are exposed to beauty the deeper our love and consciousness becomes.

The first rung on the ladder is physical beauty. I believe as we watched the sunset in anticipation for our hike I experienced this first degree of love. Anna Leah was an angel in my heaven. Everything around me oozed with quality and I was captivated by the passing seconds.

In the morning they would come to get us. I had bought a poncho and a bottle of Quetzalteca. The van picked us up along with a Brazilian couple, a Swedish hiker, a student from Amsterdam, and another couple from Germany. It began to ascend as we left the town. As we ventured further from the municipal center the poverty of the surrounding area became more apparent. Many times the van sounded like it wasn't going to make it. But it did and we kept climbing. Acatanango is thirteen thousand feet above sea level. If I had to guess we did the first five thousand by car. When we arrive at ground control we are met by two other vans. There is a father and his two young sons from Texas. They are backpacking all of Central America. There was a group of englishmen who are here on their gap year. They smoked weed and listened to music the whole hike up. They didn't make one good decision on the whole journey. There are two Chinese kids who did computer programing in Philly. A group of girls from the southern part of Belgium, a small town really. A French couple (who I think were trying to swing with me and Anna Leah [I may have been open to it, but Anna Leah didn't pick up on it]) and a French martial arist/videographer who lives in Costa Rica.

As we began on this journey we were met with animals. At the base camp were puppies who would one day be mountain dogs. Here I experienced the next rung on Diotima's ladder. Beauty of souls. To appreciate the love in terms of connecting in a spiritual way. I was encountering strangers who were here for more or less the same reason I was there. We were searching for something beyond ourselves. Our common mission of self exploration provided solace; a rich and beautiful connection that went beyond the few words we spoke to one another. The young dogs were pure innocence. The older dogs were experienced and stoic.

There was only four guides making the ascent with us. They said if at any point you are alone follow the dogs for they know the way. Every emotion I was experiencing was rising like dough becoming bread.

In the beginning we cut through a coffee farm (the volcanic ash makes very rich soil), where the horses were strong and disciplined. As I experienced more of the rungs on the ladder I felt myself expanding. There is consciously incompetent and unconsciously incompetent. Consciously competent and unconsciously incompetent. Consciously competent and unconsciously competent. As I ascended the volcano, I ascended in love and through love ascended in degrees of consciousness. This hike that now having passed the coffee farms and entered the rainforest was deeply spiritual. In the rainforest a fog began to obscure our view. We stopped for lunch and coffee. The dogs ate our bones and we kept climbing. The twelve year old was leading the group and Anna leah and I were second to last with only the Brazilians behind us. Neither couple knew what we were getting ourselves into. As we hiked I began to befriend the mountainmen. Everyone I was with was doing it for the same reason as I but these guys were doing this hike a couple times a week. I was fascinated by these real life Sysiphusian philosophers. As they began to hand out plastic for the rain (the reason our tickets were so cheap is because it was rainy season in Guatemala) I told one of them, he had a golden tooth and machete strapped to his pack, that his career was madness and he responded that "El camino es dificil pero de no caminar es mas dificil.". The walk is difficult but to not walk is more difficult. I ate a banana and persevered. The rain became more intense as the rainforest became more desolate. Slowly but surely our surroundings became nothing but volcanic ash. The fog became thicker and the rain came down harder. We were six hours into our hike and there was no going back.

We were at the spectacular mercy of the laws of nature. The next rung on Diotima's ladder is the beauty of laws. There was no doubting I was there. My fear was expressing itself in the form of awe. I was dumbstruck by nature and all of it's force. Along with the rain and the fog there was a distant grumble of eruptions from our majestic Volcan de Fuego. Anna Leah was at her breaking point. She looked back at me and shouts "I love you." as tears began to stream. Being present for her healing released such a bouquet of emotions within me. Yet a shadow loomed over me. I didn't think I love you too. I didn't think I love myself. I thought, I hate who I am right now. It's only through love that such a realization can occur. To embrace the unwanted or undesirable. That thought alone would leave me stumped for the whole trip.

Where was I? Who was I? The landscape became so desolate that I described the experience in my journal the next day as traversing into the unconscious. As we hiked further into the stom my understanding deepened. Each passing second was a revelation of love and fear. Now, I truly appreciated the beauty of laws. Here you are with all your vulnerability and all your fear. You have no say here. All we had was hope that we'd make it through the night. When we got to base camp the rain had let up for a little bit. We were the second to last to arrive. I immediately went up to where the fire was being started and tried to get dry. Anna Leah had slipped away into our tent. Maybe twenty minutes later she came up as I was telling the French martial artist and the southern Beligian girls what I did and what I studied. The Frenchman offered me a cigarette, I don't smoke those but I figured why not. He then said, "Ahhh fee loso fee. What izz love? What izz joy? Maybe tonight, we drink and discover zee universe?". Anna Leah smiled at me. She didn't say it but I could tell she was proud I was making friends. The Swedish hiker was fucking annoying though. "Dah I am the best hiker here! I got up furst!". It took us a while to get the fire going because the wood was wet. Eventually me and one of the Belgian girls got it to turn on. She had the bluest eyes I have ever seen.

Anna Leah was missing again. They were getting the food going when I went to check on her. She said she was just laying down because she was tired. I then left the sheet metal shack that the tents were in and there was a small group restrapping their boots. I began to translate for the guides. "If you want to get a closer look of Volcan de Fuego we are contractually obligated to take you. Don't let the rain stopping fool you, a storm is coming in. We do not think we should do this extra two hours of a hike. We should just go in the morning with the rest of the team as planned. Again, if you want to go we must take you. We recommend that you rent head lamps off of us." One of the Chinese kids decided to go. The German girl. The Texans. And all the English kids. The Texans, the German girl, and the Chinese kid all rented head lamps. The English kids said their phones had flashlights. Like I said they didn't make a single good decision.

Maybe an hour after they left it began to get dark. I was letting Anna Leah rest as I drank and got to know the people on the hike. The whole time we were up there we couldn't see the volcano. At one point you could make out the outline through the clouds, but it remained just there. So close and yet so far. Thunder and eruptions sound the same, the only difference is the floor would shake for eruptions. <u>My life seemed so adventurous when I had sqwabbled down to nothing.</u>

When it started to get dark the slop began to be served. I ran down to get Anna Leah. I helped her out of the tent, she looked very weak. As we began to climb the hill to the tent with the fire pit, she began to throw up. She looked at me and I saw it in her eyes. She had altitude sickness. No reason for concern, they said if anyone was feeling nauseous just to let them know. I didn't want to make a scene, she would have hated that. I tried to feed her some slop, not much went down. Then I helped her back down the hill and into the tent. Then I went up to the one guide who stayed behind and let him know that my girlfriend was unwell. "Remal.", I said with conviction. He looked at me with panic. He told me the medication was in the pack taken by one of the other guides. Two hours had passed, the rain had really picked up, and it was getting darker by the second. I told him to call for me when they got back. I went and laid down next to her. The paranoia crept in with the white noise created by the flapping of the tarp outside against the sheet metal, the thunder, the wind, the rain, and the eruptions over took me. For three hours I trembled in fear as I spooned my feverish girlfriend. Then the mountain men came and got me. When I came out the French martial artists asked where I have been. I didn't answer. The rain was really coming down now and the darkness was consuming. They gave me an anti-nausea pill and I ran to give it to Anna Leah. I do not believe it was FDA approved. I laid back down next to her. The next thing I hear is the commotion of everyone getting back to base camp.

    They are all soaking wet, covered in mud, and freezing cold. I hear the Chinese kid cry to his friend that he is scared. I had nothing left, so I began to pray. I am not religious but I was desperate. To whoever is listening get all of us off this mountain safely and I will be your slave. I am at your mercy. The noise only got louder and louder. But eventually Anna Leah stopped shaking and I was able to sleep a little. I woke up due to a nightmare. The nightmare was just red. The fiery color of it. The piercing sound of it. When I got up it was morning and the storm had passed. The sky was clear and the air was silent. You could hear the chirping birds in the distance. And before us was Volcan de Fuego. It could be seen clearly alongside it's eruptions. In the salvation of this moment tears began to well in my eyes. I had ascended to the final rung in the ladder. The beauty of the forms. This is when you appreciate beauty for the sake of beauty. The forms being the ideal verision of a given thing. This can only exist in the imagination. And because we couldn't see the volcano the whole time the day before it's absence became a presence. Until this morning when it's presence was it's presence and it exceeded expectations. I ran back in and got Anna Leah. She had fully recovered. On our descent she said that my love healed her but I think it was the anti-nausea medication. We watched the Volcano and drank coffee as a group. The dogs that had hidden underneath the sheet metal shack (it was slightly elevated off the floor) came out and allowed us to pet them. Our descent down the volcano with the view we missed yesterday now felt that we were, "Like drops of frozen rainbow light" (10) and that "God is joy and joy is God," (10). Like in the Wandering of Oisin, we had wandered into a forbidden realm and defied death. For us it was only a moment, but it could have been a life time. For Oisin it was a lifetime, but could have been a moment. As we descended with a wide landscape in view, that shadow of fear and self hate loomed. I had thought it and now I cannot unthink it. What did my nightmare mean?

We descended the volcano and made it back in to town early. We got a massive plate of food to eat and then went to get tattoos. She got a woman blooming out of a rose. Her eyes are blinded by butterflies. I got the skull of a gaucho to commemorate: Memento Mori. The next day we were having coffee and reading our books. A man recognized what I was reading and we sparked up a conversation. He was a local philosopher and in little company. We spoke about Wettgenstein and Nietzche. Then we spoke about death as he displayed his chest to me. There was a large vertical scar down the middle. He had flat lined three separate instances in his life. Each time having the same out of body experience. He left his surgical career and began to dedicate his life to philosophy in search of explanations. We exchanged numbers and later that evening he gifted me a copy of his book, "Desde umbral del la muerte". Upon the threshold of death. It is a goal of mine to translate this book to English.

The next day we left for Lake Atitlan. Here we would speak to indigenous peoples in our equally broken spanish. Through our conversations with the women we discovered, "Research has linked Guatemala's relatively high Indigenous maternal mortality ratio (MMR) to home births [3]. Indigenous women in Guatemala suffer an MMR more than twice that of their non-Indigenous counterparts (166 vs. 78)." (11) Despite the influx in tourism and immigration to these lake villages. Daddy's money goes far, but not far enough. But I was there judging others for doing the same thing I was doing. "To be a mass tourist, for me, is to become a pure late-date American: alien, ignorant, greedy for something you cannot ever have, disappointed in a way you can never admit. It is to spoil, by way of sheer ontology, the very unspoiledness you are there to experience, It is to impose yourself on places that in all non-economic ways would be better, realer, without you. It is, in lines and gridlock and transaction after transaction, to confront a dimension of yourself that is as inescapable as it is painful: As a tourist, you become economically significant but existentially loathsome, an insect on a dead thing." (12). As my existential value was being weighed, the question again began to rise in me, what is the role of the poet? The responsibility? When there is so much suffering in the world, where do we begin? How do we help without being the cause of damage in another direction? Wilde argues that if there is a social function it is separate from the act and the art itself. That art has purely aesthetic functions and those are to be recognized in the making of art, therefore the exploration of the self and atomic nuances that make us, us. As I continued to write I felt the intuitive value of self exploration. I was healing as I revealed myself through words. Yet I also found value in allowing someone else to fall in love with my words.

I came back to New York so full and yet so empty. My vocation felt more like a chore and yet the fruitful experiences continued to come. I debated a young girl who was contemplating suicide. She just wanted someone to listen. We debated, she took the position of death and I life. Our conclusion was similar to the conclusion from the film, "The Taste of Cherry". An Iranian film about a man who is in search for someone to burry him after he has committed suicide. His interactions continue to spark hope and doubt into the main characters mind. I met a physicist from Norway. A communist from Boston. And on and on. But my experience in Guatemala had hallowed me out and in it's space the looming fear and self hate began to grow.

The paranoia began to set in as I took on new challenges in my fall semester. I took Philosophy of Religion and Philosophy of Knowledge which were putting into perspective the questions I was asking. At the same time I took an intro to literature course and a poetry workshop. I was beginner at the things I loved. These classes weren't the cause of my paranoia, rather they were what was holding me together. The paranoia was a result of two or three dangerous encounters in the park. The shock of our hike. And my intense questioning of my placement in the universe. Prior to the hike I believed redefining progress was my philosophical duty, now back home I didn't know anything. I posted this poem one day while in the park:

"On the road to self discovery"

Who was I
When the world denied me
My face
Who was I when
I was hurting
And expressed it as —
But who I was
Is gone
Today is here
Lost in the monolith

Of planetary maternity
Lost in the shadows
Of who I have been
Who was I
When I found
Who I am

    I was losing myself in New York to paranoia and an obsession of writing. I was easily agitated and had little patience.
    When things were really bad (around September 2022 and October 2022) I believed I was being followed. My best guess was FBI but any of the central intelligence agencies could be at play. I had no agenda. I just wanted to write, now I am in the pursuit of a reason to write. What is my cause? Who do I write for? My answer, two years ago, while in my parents backyard is that I write for nobody. Nobody was me. He was a good guy. That wasn't gonna cut it. Do I represent New Yorkers? But I am from Westchester; the suburbs. Do I represent Latinos? But Uruguyans are of recent European decent. My skin is too fair. I am not white, but I am not Latino either. I know, I represent the middle class! But I am barely making by and I am priviledged. My parents kept helping me back up as I repeatedly fall. My doom scrolling on social media and amazon purchases are holding me back. I was a mentally unsound man child running around New York trying to help and for that I am under attack. Not actually under attack, just my imagination has gotten too good. It works in my favor when I am at the park but it works against me when I am in Grand Central.
    When I was a kid I had moments where I was a bully. That's mainly from the unresolved trauma of being bullied. Middle school at a predominately Irish classroom in a Roman Catholic school was rough for us hispanic/not-hispanic kids. It was rough for all of us. We were all a little cruel. We were all a little hurt. We had fun along the way too. My questions of placement in this world come from deep seated insecurities.

I crumbled so fast it is still hard to make sense of it. Sometimes you need a break down for a break through. At least that's what I have been told. One day, Anna Leah and I are really on the fence. I have been staying at my parents house, but now she is in Puerto Rico with her mother. I am hoping her trip helps us work past what we are going through. But it wasn't her that was the problem. It's me. I am the one putting stress on the relationship. I think it's because I can't see if she sees it my way. Her and I were best friends then suddenly every second together didn't make sense. It was my fault. I was so blind as to how it was my fault, but I was the problem. Fear, loneliness, and my imagination overtook me. The final straw was this concert I went to with Pootie Tang while she was away. It was in Harlem and was an art gallery first. But everything was considered. The videos being played. The art on the wall. The music was psychological warfare. The images on the screen were distrubing. We were immersed in the sublime. I flushed the toilet and a shower head turned on. The door said "push" but you needed to pull.

Then was the performance. KeiyaA came on to a stage that looked like her living room. She was so comfortable in the mayhem she was creating. We were all sitting on the floor and the speakers were enormous. It's the most important performance I have seen to date. I felt like I was being brainwashed and that fear made me alive to how fucking out of my mind I was. When I took the train home from Harlem that night I was too distraught to put my headphones in. I rode the train in silence thinking over what I had just witnessed. I wanted to go up to her after the show and warn her about allowing herself to lose it like that. The danger of creating art that way. "Those who go beneath the surface do so at their peril." (7). The next day I woke up and had the apartment to myself. I got stoned and watched The French Dispatch. Then I watched a short film called Opal. After I set up my typewriter at my desk and wrote a ten part poem. My guess is I was experiencing psychosis while writing it because it is one draft and manic as ever. I say things I don't even agree with but they are out on the page. The title of the poem is "Tomorrow will be yesterday". The poem is pure exploration. The good, the bad, and the ugly.

I moved back home to my parents shortly thereafter. Anna Leah and I couldn't make it work. I was the one who ended things. Not because I didn't lover her, she just wasn't believing me when I was telling her I was being followed. That she was probably being followed too. One of the final things I said to her is, "if you don't believe me than I can't protect you". In reality, the only thing she needed protection from was me. That poor woman loved me so deeply and all I did in exchange was confuse and hurt her. On top of everything I was struggling with facets of my sexuality that I still don't fully understand. I wish I could take it all back and start fresh with her, but in my process of healing I have moved on. If you are reading this, I am so sorry.

In terms of leaving busking behind there were a few reasons. The first, was obviously my deteriorating mental health. The next big reason is I felt enslaved to it. I began to feel like the hunger artist from the short story by Kafka. In the hunger artist, our main character fasts for extended periods of time. As he receives less notoriety, he begins to push the length of time in which he fasts. Until he is completely forgotten in his cage. He has this final interaction, "'I always wanted you to admire my fasting,' said the hunger artist. 'We do admire it,' said the overseer, affably. 'But you shouldn't admire it,' said the hunger artist. 'Well then we don't admire it,' said the overseer, 'but why shouldn't we admire it?' 'Because I have to fast, I can't help it,' said the hunger artist… 'because I couldn't find the food I liked. If I had found it, believe me.. I should have made no fuss and stuffed myself like you or anyone else." (13). I couldn't stop writing and this felt like it was tampering with my freedom. We look to the artist to be a source of freedom and I was not free. So I was a contradiction. A fraud. Disingenuous. I had to quit. I had to stop starving myself and find something I liked to eat. Wilde would say I had became too concerned with the social function of art. That by concentrating on the wrong function, on the social instead of the deeply personal, I lost my way. That is what precisely happened. I was engaging with fantasies beyond belief and I was miserable in my reality of writing hundreds of poems about squirrels.

When I moved back home, the boundaries between myself and my parents didn't exist. They were overstepping in every possible way. Attempting to help me when I didn't ask. A month before I was an independent artist and now I was being treated as if I was a helpless child again. I wanted to be left alone, so I can create in peace. Instead of asking me if anything was wrong they assumed that my self isolation meant I wasn't doing okay. In truth, I was managing the break up well and since I stopped writing I had picked up the habit of painting. Painting felt like a very natural transition for me. "Painting is silent poetry, and poetry is painting that speaks." (14). Again, I was making it up as I went. With no technical understanding or even ability. My philosophy towards it was to just move. I was showing up to class in November and December with paint on my hands and stains on my shirts. I began to obsess and in those two months I made close to sixty paintings.

I love my parents very deeply. They have provided so much for me over the years. The greatest gift they have given me is the ability to fail. But I had just experienced the most transformative year of my life and they were trying to box me into the idea they had of me. Instead of trying to get to know the person I had become. That alongside my unwavering paranoia and the madness inducing characteristic of painting, my deterioration was increasing at a fast rate. About half way through January I made an awful decision. I had stopped journaling all together. Now this ability to write was pent up inside me with no outlet. My only creative outlet was painting and I had run out of money for canvases. All I was doing now was reading, "The sources of the self" by Charles Taylor, "The Tibetan Book of the Dead", and meditating for long periods of time. When the semester started up again I was concentrating on questions such as, "If freedom isn't for everyone is it truly free?" "If freedom ends out our borders, is it truly freedom?" "If progress is erosive then what does that mean for our future?". I have a bit of a savior complex and I was trying to use the insights I had developed to save the world through writing. A bit dramatic but this is where I was at, but in reality I was trying to reestablish an ideal. In the poem, Tintern Abbey, by William Wordsworth, the poet is turning towards nature to reestablish an ideal that he lost in the violence that proceeded the French revolution. I think I was doing the same as I tried tackling the philosophical questions I was raising. Instead of turning toward nature I was turning towards theory. I had lost faith in the direction of society as developments in Artificial Intelligence were becoming of use for the public and I was holding out hope that artists were still the future of writing and artistry.

I was left in a cross roads, then something strange happened to me.

"Empty your heart of it's mortal dream…We come between him and the deed of his hand, we come between him and the hope of his heart." (15). In this poem we explore the mortality of reality and the immortality of fantasy. The immortal fantasy comes between the person and action. The immortal fantasy comes between the person and desire. My ability to fantasize outgrew my ability to cope with reality. Along with crippling paranoia I was experiencing intense social anxiety. Being anywhere beside my desk at home felt naked. I need to cultivate my aesthetic self again by creating for creation sake, but I have gassed myself out with all the painting. While this is going on, I became deeply immersed in a fantasy of love that blurred the lines between what was real and what was going on in my head.

Why is he looking at me? Can he hear my thoughts? Why can't I remember if I always have been able to read minds? Are the people reading my mind also whipping my memory? That birds on the branch for over an hour. Is it spying on me? Probably China or Russia. Across the street my neighbor has something orange in the window. It's probably a video camera. I lower the blinds just in case. I prefer dark rooms either way. What is progress? Why does it feel like it's design is self destructive? My parents don't care about me. I am nothing but a bad investment. My brothers have moved on. I can't trust any of my friends. Who knows who they are working for and what they are trying to get out of me? I was living like this for close to six months.

In the Sorrows of Young Werther, a novel by Ghoethe, Werther a young artist leaves his job of diplomacy and the city, opting for the country and painting. He soon meets Charollete, or Lotte, and her fiance Albert. At first he is in denial, but eventually he is overcome by his love for Charollete that it becomes unbearable. He moves back to the city but life as a diplomat just doesn't agree with him. He returns back to the country and to Charollete. He knows Charollete can never love him back but he is desperate. It eventually becomes clear that Charollete is toying with him. Our artist stops creating art and only creates a fantasy. He is not in love with Charollete, he is love with an idea. He aesthesizes her beyond compare. The book ends with Werther tragically shooting himself in the head.

I mention this story because of what happens next in my story. I developed out of desperation and admiration a fantasy of someone that could never acknowledge me the way I cared for them. Like Werther I was in love with the idea of a person without being able to realize who they actually were. Then on the last Wednesday of January 2023, I read a poem titled "High time I did something brave" at Bowery Poetry Club. This reading filled me with a wide array of emotions and I left walking two inches above the ground. I was finally acknowledged by this person and my euphoria only grew.

The next day I bought a massive canvas. I was going to name it "Anna Leah". My family was away in Uruguay and them returning was draining me of my serotonin. Being home alone had temporarily returned the independence that I had longed for. I lay the canvas down on the floor of my room and began to circle it. I would slash droplets of paint like a priest anointing a casket with holy water. The result was an immense outpouring and as I gazed upon it I understood what I needed to do. I was to kill myslef. This painting will be my note. I propped it up on the easel. Then I knelt in the square where the canvas once was. An eclectic color surrounding it's borders. I took off my shirt and cut the bun out of my hair. I then took the knife and turned it on my belly. Yeat says, "It knows not what it is; and gather me Into the artifice of eternity." (16) in his poem, Sailing to Byzantium. In the poem, he describes a youthful love. The type of love where you know everything. In the next stanza he describes a dwindling man and longing for eternity. It's only in the third stanza that he expresses the desire to die so that he may, "Consume my heart away; sick with desire and fastened to a dying animal.". Is this destiny of the poet? To strive to be one with the art they are creating. As I stared at the painting and contemplated death, my dog licked my cheek. I dropped the knife and began to cry. I got up and began to destory everything I owned. I shaved my head and my beard. Packed up books, my camping gear, and some food. I named the painting that was going to transcend my mortal life into an immortal one, "Seppuku". Then I left. With no intention of coming back. Got in my truck with my dog and began to drive south. When my brothers discovered what I had done to my room they raced after me. I was in North Carolina for a day by myself. Then my younger brother spent three days with me. My older brother spent the morning and then he needed to get back to work.

    He slipped me some cash and told me to stay for however long that could get me, but to make sure I came back. I had told them my plan was to drive to Guatemala and work on the volcano. I stayed another four nights in North Carolina. The first three it rained all day and all night. There was a trail through the swamp that I'd take my dog to when the weather let up for a few minutes. One day I saw crane come down on to the water. It gently dragged it's claw on top of the bay. Just enough so the nail went in. Suddenly, I am in a pool or a tub. My dad is infront of me. His hair is dark and his skin has no wrinkles. He drags his finger in the water and splashes it on to my face.

Why we remember somethings and not other is hard, but sometimes when memories occur is a more difficult question. Here I am talking with groundskeeper and watching the sunset. This crane comes in and now I am thinking of my father. He came to this country with next to nothing and I could be his third son to graduate from college. I have to get back. I am only a semester away.

That night it dropped down to sixteen degrees. My dog and I were wrapped in sleeping bags and blankets. The next morning I woke up, started the fire, threw the coffee on, and began to pack up. By the time the coffee was done, my truck was loaded, my dog was in the car. I sipped on it slowly taking one last look at the campgrounds around me. The oranged thin leaves from pine trees. Pine trees that were dropping pines with loud thuds. All night, listening to the thumps and owls in the distance.

My sister in law sent me $100 and so did my best friend. I filled my tank and bought some beef jerky that I split with my dog. I was heading south. I chased the sun as I drove down that open road. I got to Daytona beach at one in the morning. I parked at Walmart and slept in the car. My alarm went off at four am and we went back over to the beach. When we walked on to the beach the sun was just beginning to rise. We laid down in the warm sand and listened to the ocean. I sat up and stared at the waves. Where does one begin and the other end? I had been reading Basho and Calvino.

From there I visited my brother in Tennessee. Slept two nights and then went back to New York. I read my poem "Tomorrow will be yesterday" at Bowery Poetry Club on the first Wednesday of March. The next day I took a vow of silence. I wasn't eating. I just felt so alive without it. Time was my nutrition. By not speaking or eating I was desperately tyring to control elements of my life that had slipped through my grasp. My family intervened with the best of intentions, but to this day I can't— I have forgiven them but whenever I reflect on this time I can't shake this feeling of betrayal. I was in therapy. I had sought out help. What I needed was time and space. These seemed to be commodities they could not grant me. I meditated in the backyard in my underwear, the sun bleaming down made me cry cool tears of bliss, and my parents didn't understand. They called the councilling center and told them they were scared. That they didn't know what I would do. What I was capable of. When I got to campus a detective was waiting for me. There was an ambulance brought on to campus and I walked into the back of it with a smile on my face. <u>The confusion of this time period has brought everything up from our pasts. Nobody did the right thing, but I am the only one who has been willing to take accountability. My siblings have acted immaturily and advantegously. My parents have been petty and manipulative. The entire sequence of events has left me terribly alone. I am at peace.</u>

Then I was all alone again. Probably more alone then I have ever been. I was advocating for myself and the doctors were writing it off as mania. Prescribing me medication after two minute conversations. Your only option is complacency. Luckily a week in it became abundantly clear that this was a circus of misfits. The psychiatric unit is filled with failed and aspiring writers. Each person was a kindred spirit. I hated being medicated, but my hatred was outweighed by a tremendous sense of belonging. Nobody was pretending to be healthier then they were. We wore our hurt on our sleeves and everyone understood. When I got out a month later, I operated like the main character from the french film, "The Pickpocket". All my movements were considered caused by a crushing anxiety that overcame me. I was no longer in the world of misfits, I was back in the world of misfits pretending everything is okay. I decided to disappear. To lock myself away in the basement of my parents house. I was to write continuously. <u>Little did I know the ways in which I was retraumatizing myself repeatedly.</u> But I was sitting at my computer or at my poetry journal getting a very few words out a time. It was really difficult to stay head strong but I did. Persevering, remembering the words of the mountainman, "El camino es dificl pero de no caminar es ma dificil.". I ended up finishing the first draft of my novel, One More Cup of Coffee. I went back out to Central Park a handful of times to prove that I still have the "mana". Life force.

Now, I write this essay, exploring my experience, to find the answer of what is the role of the poet in society? Perhaps to answer the question we must explore, what is art or poetry? And to answer that we may need to explore the artistic impulse or the desire to create.

Poetry, when done in the pursuit of spontaneity and inspiration, captures the essence of a moment and now something fleeting has become eternal. Engaging with literature from an educational perspective has two fold benefits. The first is that it expands the consciousness by creating a lively imagination. The second is that it makes the students literate, worldly, and better citizens. In Culture and Anarchy by Mathew Arnold, art is expressed as the search for perfection. Because art has such a large influence on the public, poets are the unrecognized legislators of the world, Arnold argues that it must contain social function. How was I utilizing this function by creating art in public? If art has a social function, then how much should the artist consider the audience when creating? Some may argue that the function of art is to be created and nothing more. Others, such as Arnold will have the artist putting an emphasis on their message and social impact.

Walter Pater when talking about the function of art, in the conclusion of The Renassiance, says, "To burn always with this hard, gemlike flame, to maintain this ecstasy, is success in life." (17) Pater believes that through the passions we find the intervals of consciousness. That art has no moral or social obligations, but purely aesthetic ones. Or at least not one in it's consummation. While busking I struggled with this notion. I was bearing witness to how my work was effecting others and would weigh my impact to a fault. Are we beginning to see how much pressure the poet has? How much power the words can convey in a social setting? How much they can effect the poet and their mental well being?

So, we have Wilde and Pater who believe that art is, to be, and that it serves no social function. That we should surround ourselves with art to refine our intuition and expand our consciousness. Arnold believes that art has social and moral obligations. Now, I have put myself in the position where I have done both. I have gone out to the streets and written poems for strangers. Asking myself, "One, do they know the truth? Two, do they deserve to know the truth? Three, do I have the right to tell them?". What the truth was varied from person to person. There are only three objective truths, as far as I can tell, and that is that we all love, we all suffer, and we will all die. When I wrote for others I'd always try to be present to one of these three notions. I have written entirely for myself. I have begun to jot down ideas in my poetry notebook again. And I have completed my first novel. Until I edit it and find a way to publish, that work is completely for my own pleasure. Same with all the paintings I have made. My actions in the last year suggest that I agree more with Wilde and Pater. My time as a busker would have leaned more towards Mathew Arnold.

Each piece of art has a unique value or quality. In the beginning of this essay I suggested that art is the transition of potential into quality or value. Value is probably the more accurate term, but I have a personal preference toward quality. Art can also be considered to be the interpretation of the imagination by the imaginer. I have an image in my head, which leads me to plan out a work on the canvas, but no matter how talented I am, the piece won't match my imagination. Perhaps that is why I create so vigorously. The same could be said about poems. Poetry at it's best emulates moments, by making them last longer as you read a poem. Had I gone through with it. Let's say I committed seppuku that day and my blood splattered over the canvas. Would the painting contain my lifetime or my final moment? Is it the value of my being or of my death? Is it just the interpretation of the anguish I was putting myself through? The right and wrong answer is that it's probably a little bit of everything.

In my time as a poet in Central Park, I'd tell you that art is potential becoming quality or value. And the transition mirrored itself in the reader. Meaning that the potential in me became quality they interact with the quality and it creates potential in them. Internal to external to external to internal. Potential to quality to quality to potential. Similar to Socrates's iron link and his chain of divine inspiration.

The question of one's own potential being finite used to frighten me a great deal. My conclusion is that everything is an extension of consciousness. That our senses interact with the world and we experience the conscious organization of reality and not reality itself. The essence of a thing can be what it is capable of based off our past experiences. We use past experiences to assign potential. This is what gives it's quality or value. Since all things are an extension of consciousness, then that means the potential that surrounds you is the potential within you. As long as you're present then you can never run out of potential. Ones individual potential is as infinite as the passing seconds.

If we consider this to be what art is then we must side with Arnold. If art is unlocking potential in the recipient the artist ought to be responsible for the moral implications of their work. But I am still not convinced. My time painting tells me that art is more the interpretation of the imagination. My time as a novelist says the same. And to be a voice amongst the masses you have an obligation to capture your imagination as it comes. When we begin to filter for approval we dampen the authenticity of our ability and truth. It's only in exploring every nook and cranny with our words do we actualize the most authentic version of ourselves. This is the truest way to love yourself. Is to make art that explores yourself in search of resolution. Resolution for whatever burden we are all carrying. Fear of aging. Fear of dying. Fear of being loved. Fear of being forgotten. If we continue from Arnold's position, your social function is in being one of the many faceted voices of your time. You are helping to paint the picture by adding perspective. Authentic perspective. It's imperative that it is authentic because your imagination is in you but not of you. To be living in the modern world means to be a producer and product of culture.

My biggest problem with art being the interpretation of the imagination, is it separates an individual. Art in many ways is the synthesis of ideas and emotions. If we come together in the act how come when explaining it we separate the act. We have the imaginer and the interpreter, but they are one in the same. Couldn't the art be the coming together of imagination and interpretation, something more fluid then a chain of causation. Poetry is smoother than that, it's like rollerblading. But then again, other times it's like chewing rocks.

Both of these definitions, potential to quality and interpretation of the imagination, contain something in common and that is they can be reduced to a singular definition. That definition being, the manipulation of matter in order to create something out of nothing. This definition fits as an explanation of art that has social functions and art that does not. My quarrel with this definition is it is too inclusive. Under this definition the way I place my fork next to my plate could be considered art. The way I walk is art. The way I breathe, the way I see, the way I dance, the way I sit in class, the way I listen, and drink my coffee could all be considered art. Any instance in which there is movement that causes any sort of change would be considered art. I suppose this is the lure of modern art. It challenges the degrees in which we consider art to be art.

One time I went to the MOMA in NYC. I was captivated by the works of Basquiat and Pollock. <u>I am a shallow geek. I know the works that speak to me and the names I should know, but I am no consiur. I am, when it comes to all things, a passionate amateur.</u> At some point I ended up in a room filled with different paintings and a crowd had formed in the corner. I made my way over and saw a gray square painted on the white wall. The description to the right describes, "an array of use in colors to capture the wide range of human anguish". That's when I realized the people were taking pictures of where a painting used to be. They must have repainted the walls and painted around the painting while it was still there. Then when they removed the painting the old paint remained. When we have a definition of art that is as inclusive as the manipulation of matter to create something out of nothing, we have no system to gauge the value of art. In this example old paint in a square drew a crowd taking pictures of literally nothing. If we want a definition of art that allows us to value it then we have to think beyond art just being the manipulation of matter. If we are to truly consider this as a definition for art we must find a way to differentiate the value of art.

Depth of artistry, a square of old paint to a Picasso, suggests that art can be measured in degrees. I would separate different art into three degrees. The first degree is profound art. Profound art is art that contains beauty in which we recognize our own mortality. Recognition in this instance comes in the form of gratitude for the fleeting moment of beauty in which we are engaged.

The second category of art is the sublime. Sublime art is art that contains odious characteristics in which we recognize our own mortality. Both the profound and the sublime make us recognize our own mortality. In effect, they both cause change in the viewer of the art. The way they cause change is what differentiates the two. The profound does so through apparent beauty, while the sublime does so through subliminal beauty. For this reason sublime pieces of art require more work to interpret, while the profound art's interpretation is within the experience of experiencing it. The profound and the sublime are equal in form.

The third degree of artistry takes on a lesser form, and this artistry is good and bad art. This is art that is systematic and lacks creativity. Good and bad art causes no change in the viewer. Good art evokes momentary pleasure. While bad art evokes nothing or disdain. All three degrees of art remain with us in some way after the experience has ended. This is why it is important to engage with art that challenges us. If we consider art to be the manipulation of matter in order to make something out of nothing, then our very way of being is an act of artistry. By engaging with art that is profound or sublime, the artistry of our being is enhanced and refined. If engaging with only good and bad art, then a reflection of good and bad will be emulated in the way we view the world.

I return to the definitions offered up earlier. Why can't both be right? Wilde and Pater identify a type of artistry that is deeply personal and refines intuition or the soul. While Arnold refers to an art with moral and has social functions. This type of art is less personal and conforms authenticity. The perks of taking this route is it may gain for you fiscally and in notoriety. The one identified by Wilde and Pater, will expand your consciousness and refine your intuition. Allowing you to be more sensitive to the wide array of potential and emotions we are surrounded by. The down side is this is the route I took when I began to lose my mind. Self-exploration is necessary to actualize yourself, but exploration in excess can blur the lines between reality and fantasy, as we saw in Werther and my almost demise.

It's a a very mathematical position to think you have to pick. The reality of it is the poet's role in society is to do a combination of both. To interpret their imagination. To transform potential into quality or value. To have obligations to themself. To also have obligations to society. The biggest problem in modern times is not knowing where to begin. One can even argue that by interpreting the imagination, potential is becoming value simultaneously.

In the Phaedrus by Plato, Socrates and a young man named Phaedrus leave the walls of Athens. Socrates asks Phaedrus to recite a speech he has recently heard from another philosopher about the nature of rhetoric. This leads to a lengthy Socratic dialogue about rhetoric and the soul. Socrates concludes his argument with the chariot metaphor. For Plato there are two worlds. We discussed the world of the forms when on the volcano and with Werther. It is the perfect world; the world of ideas. This world is eternal, unchanging, perfect, and possesses absolute knowledge. The actual world is temporary, constantly changing, imperfect and insecure. The soul is the only thing from the real world that possesses the characteristics of the ideal. It is immortal and the true source of knowledge. He states, "Of the nature of the soul, and her true from let me speak briefly and in a figure." (18). He describes the soul as being constructed by three parts. A chariot pulled by two winged horses, one black and the other light. The charioteer represents the logical or reason. This part of the soul steers the chariot, therefore guides the soul. The white horse is the spirited. Representing courage, nobility, and bravery which comes from the heart. The black is eros, the hungry, the passionate, and ignoble part of the soul. To steer the horses is a difficult task. It's only when the charioteer is able to cultivate harmony between the two wild horses that the chariot begins to ascend. When in harmony the chariot ascends into the heavens and enters the world of the ideal. The soul is able to enter the forms through divinity and the wings of the horses represent divinity, therefore wisdom, goodness, and beauty.

We can view the expression of art to mirror the nature of the soul according to Plato. Art when made to interpret the imagination is the white horse. Art made as potential becoming quality is the black horse. The artist is the charioteer. It is in finding a balance between these two expressions that the artist may ascend into the realm of the forms. Or into the depth of fantasy.

So we have decided that the poet has obligations toward society and toward themselves. I offer up a synthesis of the three definitions of art we were able to come up with. Art is the manipulation of matter to transform potential into quality via the interpretation of the imagination.

What is the position of the poet then? Perhaps it is to be overtly romantic about an ideal. To latch on to it and allow fantasy to run rampant. Following the path and along the way developing character. This almost led to my demise. Why do artists crave immortality? The fear of death is immense but what may be bigger is our fear of being forgotten. I almost died for a love I could not attain. I almost died so I could live on in my art. The countless poems and writing I had done will be eternalized in my slipping away. I'd be like Kafka never getting to witness the success of my work. This was the perfect in between. I made my art for myself. I interpreted my imagination over and over. Now it would be time for the world to see my art and my social obligation was to not be there physically but to immerse my essence in my works. I was in the pursuit of perfecting what it meant to be a poet. I had found my opportunity to ascend aesthetically. Aesthetic absolution.

I'd like to take a moment to talk about T.S. Elliot. T.S. Elliot was a modernist poet who won the Nobel Prize for Literature. His most notable work is either "The Wastelands", "Portrait of a Lady", or the poem we will be discussing today, "The Love Song of J. Alfred Prufrock". The poem begins with an Italian epigraph from Dante's "Inferno". The speaker is a character in hell revealing his secrets to Dante because nobody ever leaves where they are. The final line in the epigraph talks about fear of being shamed. Dante will eventually rise from hell and share the secrets of the man. Shame and embarrassment will be a recurring theme in the poem. In the opening stanza Eliot describes himself being in a questionable part of town. This poem is written with repetition and in a fractured style. The first example of repetition and fractures is the sudden change of describing an area in town to, "In the room the women come and go / Talking of Michelangelo."(19). This line is repeated in a mocking way. As if J. Alfred Prufrock loathes listening to their surface level discussion of art.

After the Michelangelo line, Eliot describes a yellow smog as if it were a cat rubbing his nose against the window panes. The smog lingers upon the pools, licks it's tongue into the corners of the evening, and slips away by the terrace. In the stanza that follows we see the way Prufrock lives in fantasy. "There will be time to murder and create, / And time for all the works and days of hands / that lift and frop a question on your plate; Time for you and time for me, / And time yet for a hundred indecisions, / And for a hundred visions and revisions, / Before the taking of a toast and tea." (19). This is all followed by the Michelangelo line. In this quote, we are seeing how our main character is trapped by indecision and overthinking as a result of living in fantasies. There seems to be a party that Prufrock is attending. In the poem he seems to be floating back and forth between this tea party and his imagination.

The next stanza opens with, "And indeed there will be time / to wonder, 'Do I dare?' and, 'Do I dare?' / time to turn back and descend the stair, / with a bald spot in the middle of my hair— / (They will say: 'How his hair is growing thin!')" (19). Here we see Prufrock tempting himself with action, by questioning if he "dares". Another repetition that we will see in the same stanza, he says, "Do I Dare / Disturb the universe?" (19). Does he risk engaging with the world? To track back a little bit, the line in the beginning of the stanza about his hair reveals a few things to us. The first is that our main character is insecure about his hair loss. But also that he is meant to represent the decay of mortality. He has aged and continues to age. Yet he talks about time as if he has it in abundance.

In the seventh stanza we see that Prufrock has, "measured out my life with coffee spoons." (19). This alone is a depressing notion. I think the intention behind this line is two fold. The first is that he has attended many of these tea parties that he is currently daydreaming at. The second is the immense fear of the finitude of living. To measure your life in coffee spoons probably reveals how short our existence actually is.

In the seventh and eighth stanza Prufrock is talking about how he knows the people he is surrounded by. Meaning he doesn't need to get to know their superficiality. "And I have known the arms already, known them all– / Arms that are braceleted and white and bare / (But in the lamplight, downed with light brown hair!)" (19). What we can presume from this point in the poem is that Prufrock has a vivid and vast internal reality. He won't act on any of the women that surround him because he is so attached to an ideal woman. One without any flaws and is immortal because his internal fantasy won't die the way he will. That's why when he sees beautiful arms the next thing he thinks is that in the right lighting the arms are actually hairy. All imperfections are extenuated by the perfect fantasy. No woman can compare to the woman of our dreams.

He continues describing the streets he is walking through, maybe after the tea party. He sees lonely men hanging out their windows and wishes he was a crab or a lobster crawling along the bottom of the ocean.

In the following line we get another reference to his balding head. Emphasizing this idea of decay and death. His greatness has flickered. Death has held his coat and snickered; he was afraid of this near death experience.

Again, Prufrock is questioning if the way he has spent his time to be worthwhile. He then imagines himself to be Lazarus. A biblical figure, who is brought back to life by Jesus even though his body had begun to decay. He says, "I am Lazarus, come from the dead, / Come back to tell you all, I shall tell you all —" (19). Tell us what? What the underworld was like? Even then nothing is revealed except for the fact "That is not what I meant at all; / That is not, it all." (19). Our main character is deeply misunderstood and as result has developed an elaborate internal reality. His internal reality is complete and immortal, while his external is incomplete and aging.

"I grow old…I grow old… / I shall wear the bottoms of my trousers rolled." (19), we can interpret this line as a momentary recognition of his age, then immediately trying to reclaim his youth by altering his style. In the next stanza he opens with "Shall I part my hair behind? Do I dare eat a peach?" (19). Does he cover his bald spot? Does he dare have sex? A peach being a very juicy and sensual object. Prufrock is lonely and his options surrounding him but his imagination is far greater than his reality. The next lines are, "I shall wear white flannel trousers, and walk upon the beach. / I have heard the mermaids singing, each to each. / I do not think that they will sing to me." (19). The ocean is a literary tool used to describe the unknown. Due to it's disconnect from reality and it's inability to be explored without equipment. Because Prufrock is shelled up inside himself reality itself is the unknown. And in the unknown he sees mythical creatures, that's how much distance he has put between himself and the world. In Greek mythology sirens (mermaids) would sing to tempt soldiers into the sea so that they would drown them. But even these creatures that Prufrock sees are not tempting him. The poem ends with, "human voices wake us, and we drown." (19). Prufrock has immersed himself in the unknown and it isn't until real human voices wake him that he drowns in his imagination.

I wanted to write about this poem because I am curious as to what is the artistic impulse, why do we create? Prufrock is an example of what happens when you spend too long in your imagination, but also highlights why we imagine in the first place. The starkness of our own reality, a reality in which we decay and die, is too much for some people to bear. So we immerse ourselves in our imagination as an escape, but the artist goes a step further. They attempt to bring out that internal reality into the external world in some way. Perhaps we do this because this capturing of the imagination will remain when we move on. In some way we remain through our art. We are all driven by a fear of death, but perhaps the artist is driven by the denial of death.

By engaging with art, more specifically our imaginiation, we are really engaging with immortality. Fantasy is immortal. Reality is mortal. The only problem is the fantasy isn't real. You can write love poems, but if you don't have someone to love it doesn't matter. We see this to be especially true in "The Love Song of J. Alfred Prufrock". He becomes so engaged with fantasy that he drowns in the unknown. Because to truly know something it has to be out in the world and not in our books or at museums or when that album is playing. Knowledge is found in books, wisdom is found on park benches and talking to strangers. Or on top of volcanos. Or driving across the country. Or behind a wheel barrel.

Beauty is represented by youth in stories and poems. In A.E. Housman's, "To an Athlete Dying Young" we see this idea reinforced. The poem is an ode to the star of the track team. He has died young and because of that he never will slip into the ambiguity of gloriless existence. He will never grow old and long for the good ol days. He will die long before that curroption occurs. It is better that he has died young because now his beauty will be eternal.

Arthur Schopenhaur, a German philosopher who lived during the 1800s, had a theory called the will to live. Schopenhaur was largely influenced by Eastern Philosophies and his work from 1818, "The World as Will and Representation", is regarded as his greatest. In this piece of philosophy he characterizes the phenomenal world as the manifestation of a blind and irrational will. A drive that is the origin of all desires and ambitions. That drive is a will to live. It steers the course of our life. Schopenhaur argues that to truly be free we must deny imposing this will to live on objects. One might argue that the artist or the poet, the person we look to as symbol of freedom, escaped from the mundane of regular reality, is horrifically unfree. We take objects that were nothing prior to our engagement and impose this will on it. We impose value on to something that otherwise is valueless. To be free according to Shopenhaur would be to be disconnected from objects in the physical world. Perhaps, that is why writing in the park was so liberating, I was releasing myself of the poems in the instant I wrote them. I was truly free for a moment in time.

We are still trying to solve the problem of the artistic impulse. I think back to Freud's pleasure principle. In talking about his pleasure principle he highlights the three ways in which we will suffer. Suffering from our own body because we are doomed to decay. Suffering from the external world in, "Which may rage against us with overwhelming and merciless forces of destruction." (20), and from our relations with other people. The pleasure principle is simple then. The pleasure principle dominates our mental apparatus and decides the purpose of life. "What we call happiness in the strictest sense comes from the (preferably sudden) satisfaction of needs which have been dammed up to a high degree, and it is from its nature only possible as an episodic phenomenon." (20). The pleasure principle is the main force of the id that seeks immediate gratification of all needs, wants, and urges. Freud's school of psychoanalytics divides the mind up into three parts. The Id which is essentially your immediate consciouness. The superego witch is the more logical and considered part of your consciousness. Finally, the ego which acts as a judge between the two. The Ego and superego are both slightly submerged in the unconscious. While the Id is completely unconscious.

It sounds like we are getting closer to understanding why the poet creates. Like the will to live, the pleasure principle is the hidden motivation that drives all action. The only problem is the pleasure principle seeks to to fufill our most basic and primitive urges. For example hunger, thirst, anger, and sex. Some artists, myself included, feel that creating is just as necessary as these basic urges, but in reality they can't be. Starvation and writer's block feel very similar, but despite their similarity I will not die by not being able to write.

We saw that fantasy and ideas of immortality are closely aligned. That life only really happens beyond our books. The idea of the will being imposed on objects aligns with part of our definition of art. It helped prove that artists are unfree, but it doesn't explain why they create. The pleasure principle shines a light on why people take action. To fufill basic needs and desires, to alleviate suffering in the pursuit of happiness. But this isn't a drive for all things, it's a drive for some things. Not all. We turn to an older Freud for a possible solution.

In Freud's, "Beyond the pleasure principle", Sigmund offers up the death drive. A tendency inherent in all organic beings to return to an inorganic state. Freud offers up the life drive and the death drive. They sometimes adopt the names of Eros and Thanatos after the greek gods of love and death. Again, I think about Plato's chariot from the Phaedrus. All dualities are best utilized in harmony to one another not opposition. The death drive manifests itslef self destrucively. It comes from this compulsion to repeat. Behavior being repeated that sometimes has no business being repeated. Creating art can feel like a compulsion, especially with the more time spent creating a work of art.

I fear I am getting lost in my explanation of a very simple belief of mine. I believe the drive behind all actions is a fear of dying. The one distinguishing characteristic of human consciousness and any other conscious life forms is a recognition of one's own mortality. When we understand death as children, the next thing we understand is one day it will happen to us. One could argue that this is the stage in childhood when we become self aware.

Behind every decision is this fear, more apparently so in larger decisions. In the response to this fear is where free will exists. We may choose to be complacent to the fear of dying and forfeit our freedom. Or we can act in spite of our fear. To conquer your fear is the path of righteousness and freedom.

Growing up there was a cliff jump a few miles from my house. My friends and I would go every summer. We would walk the gravel and dirt path to the bend by the tree. Then we would descend the hill to where our destiny awaited us. There was three heights. Small, medium, and "Suicide". Suicide got it's name from someone who mistimed their jump. See it was the highest point but it was also a literal point. You had to balance your foot at the peak of the rock, leap, and aim for a pocket in the water. My biggest fear then and now is heights (being buried alive is a close second). Whenever we would go to the cliff, I'd waste no time and jump straight from Suicide. Everything in my body was telling me not to jump. It was this tremendous fear of dying and that is precisely why I *needed* to jump. This is what I mean when I say to act in spite of your fear.

The artist evades this fear by engaging with the immortal fantasy. Fantasies don't die the way we do. And we create with the belief that we live on through the art. The way a parent lives on in their child. In some ways we can argue that the artist is free. I know, I just said the artist is unfree. I am developing an idea, please bear with me.

That they act in spite of their fear of death. That they are making something that defiantly outlasts them. But on the other hand we could argue that the artist is crippled by this fear of dying. That like J. Alfred Prufrock they are compulsively trapped in their imaginations.

Now let's unpack my suicide attempt. Seppuku is a violent way of ending things, but it is a noble embrace of death. There was a freedom I tasted that came as a result from the highest form of freedom there is. To die on your own terms. My terms was to transcend life and become one with my art. My blood splattering on to the canvas would be evidence of my final stroke of life. Was I compelled by a fear of dying or a fear of never having truly lived?

Almost a year after the event and I am slightly agoraphobic. I am working on it. Consistent with the work. <u>Moving to the south and being forced to become self reliant has put some fucking hair on my chest. No disrepect to those who deal with agorphobia. It was one of the most challenging things I have ever had to overcome. I still have reclusive and hermit like tendencies, but I held myself to a standard of quality of living. One that requires you to put things on the back burners. Including your fears. There is no time to be scared when you knee deep in the work.</u> Part of the work has allowed me to believe that I was compelled towards death out of fear of dying. Out of being tired of being afraid. To embrace it and proclaim, "Fuck you!" as the lights slowly dimmed. I am not a man seeking profection in his art. I am chasing freedom. True poetic freedom.

Going to a Catholic School, growing up my first insecurities came from the invasive notion of an all-knowing and all-powerful God. It became abundantly clear very early on that such a God and free will were contradictory concepts. I step out into the world wondering is there a God or am I free? The poet is free. Your actions can only be determined if you are complacent to the fear of dying. The poet spends time with the immortal. Is this in defiance of death or the escape of fear? If it is the escape of fear than you're unfree. If it is in defiance of death than you are free. How do you differentiate between the two? I believe the free poet stays loyal to their imagination and accepts that their work may not be accepted but it is undeniably original. The unfree poet compromises his message. Altering the interpretation of the imagination, opting for social value by constraining one's message. This isn't true artistry rather a pursuit of fame, wealth, or social clout.

The true artistic impulse, therefore is the pursuit of freedom. Freedom from the fear of dying. The truly free are the ones who do not compromise their imagination, while the those using art as the escape of the fear of dying only attain the illusion of freedom. Now I will give one final warning. To achieve the type of freedom I am referring to comes with a catch. That catch is immense feelings of powerlessness and isolation.

To conclude, I was a construction worker. I had a spiritual and intellectual awakening. I found poetry through the freedom of working remotely because of COVID. My friend got me a poem from Colorado. I went to Central Park with my typewriter. I moved in with Anna Leah. Jack Keroauc handed me a beer. I met a mad woman in the park. I ascended a volcano and as a result ascended in my understanding of love. I came back with a looming self hate. Paranoia began to set in. My depression, anxiety, and imagination are running out of control. Anna Leah and I break up. I move back home. Painting becomes my medium. My parents and I cannot see eye to eye. I fell in love with an idea, not a person. I read a poem and have a suicide attempt. The North Carolina wilderness became my temporary hermitage. Then Florida. Then Tennessee. Then another poem and the psychiatric unit for a month. I finished my novel, slowly but surely. The artist either has a social responsibility or doesn't or has both? We viewed art as the potential becoming quality. This is a definition of art that has social obligations. We viewed art as the interpretation of the imagination. This definition of art has no social obligations. Both these definitions of art can be reduced to the manipulation of matter to make something out of nothing. This is too inclusive, so I offered a way to measure the degrees of art. Profound and sublime art make us recognize our mortality. Good and bad art cause no change. I synthesized the three definitions of art offered thus far. The result is the manipulation of matter to transform potential into quality via the interpretation of the imagination. We then looked to J. Alfred Prufrock as a possible explanation for the artistic impulse. Inferring that fantasies are immortal and reality is mortal. I then looked to the will to live, the pleasure principle, and the death drive as possible motives for the artistic impulse. In the pursuit of an explanation we offer up a resolution for why anyone does anything. That reason is a fear of dying. That this fear is the all pervasive and ever present motivation for all action. Our freedom comes in response to that fear. We are unfree if we are complacent to that fear and allow it to dictate our actions. We are free if we stand opposed to that fear and allow it to dictate our actions in the reverse. The poet either creates as defying this fear of death by pursuing immortality or is escaping into immortality as a denial of mortality, therefore being complacent to the fear. The one who remains loyal to the imagination, as it comes, is truly free while the one who compromises their imagination is unfree. The artistic impulse, therefore in it's truest form is the pursuit of freedom. Freedom from the fear of dying. Freedom comes with a catch. By pursuing immortality through the manipulation of matter to transform potential into quality via the interpretation of the imagination. I am going to take a nap now, but before I do I will finish this essay with my favorite qoute.

"The only way to deal with an unfree world is to become so absolutely free that your very existence is an act of rebellion" (20).

This isn't my story. This is a part of my story that I wrote when I was in need of working things out. I am still knee deep in the work. I will sit and write my whole story one day, but until then I can only give episodes. Thank you for reading.

Works Cited

1. Wordsworth, William. "Lines Composed a Few Miles above Tintern Abbey,..." *Poetry Foundation*, Poetry Foundation, www.poetryfoundation.org/poems/45527/lines-composed-a-few-miles-above-tintern-abbey-on-revisiting-the-banks-of-the-wye-during-a-tour-july-13-1798. Accessed 5 Dec. 2023.
2. Fanon, Frantz, and Richard Philcox. *Black Skin, White Masks*. Penguin Books, 2021.
3. Plato, and Christopher J. Rowe. *Phaedo*. Cambridge University Press, 2001.
4. Rilke, Rainer Maria, et al. *Poetry of Rilke*. North Point Press, 2011.
5. Suzuki, Shunryū, and Trudy Dixon. *Zen Mind, Beginner's Mind*. 2005.
6. "A Quote by F. Scott Fitzgerald." *Goodreads*, Goodreads, www.goodreads.com/quotes/103751-that-is-part-of-the-beauty-of-all-literature-you. Accessed 4 Dec. 2023.
7. Nevile, Jill, and Oscar Wilde. *The Picture of Dorian Grey, Oscar Wilde*. Oxford University Press, 2000.
8. Shakespeare, William, and Harold Jenkins. *Hamlet*. Thomson Learning, 2005.
9. Kreuter, Eric A. "Prose and cons: USe of poetry in existential-humanistic therapy for prisoners." *Journal of Poetry Therapy*.
10. "The Wanderings of Oisin: Book I - Poem by William Butler Yeats." *Back to Main Page*, famouspoetsandpoems.com/poets/william_butler_yeats/poems/10410. Accessed 4 Dec. 2023.
11. Olivas, Elijah T., et al. "Reducing Inequities in Maternal and Child Health in Rural Guatemala through the CBIO+ Approach of Curamericas: 6. Management of Pregnancy Complications at

Community Birthing Centers (Casas Maternas Rurales) - International Journal for Equity in Health." *BioMed Central*, BioMed Central, 28 Feb. 2023, equityhealthj.biomedcentral.com/articles/10.1186/s12939-022-01758-6#:~:text=Research%20has%20linked%20Guatemala's%20relatively,78)%20%5B4%5D.

12. Wallace, David Foster, et al. *Consider the Lobster*. Ascensius Press, 2011.
13. Kafka, Franz, and Nahum Norbert Glatzer. *The Complete Short Stories of Franz Kafka*. Vintage, 2005.
14. "A Quote by Plutarch." *Goodreads*, Goodreads, www.goodreads.com/quotes/7401272-painting-is-silent-poetry-and-poetry-is-painting-that-speaks. Accessed 4 Dec. 2023.
15. "The Host Is Riding from Sidhe." *Genius*, genius.com/4361521. Accessed 4 Dec. 2023.
16. Yeats, William Butler. "Sailing to Byzantium by William Butler Yeats." *Poetry Foundation*, Poetry Foundation, www.poetryfoundation.org/poems/43291/sailing-to-byzantium. Accessed 4 Dec. 2023.
17. Pater, Walter. "The Renaissance ." *Conclusion*, victorianweb.org/authors/pater/renaissance/conclusion.html. Accessed 4 Dec. 2023.
18. Plato. *Phaedrus*. Giardini, 1975.
19. Eliot, T. S. "The Love Song of j. Alfred Prufrock by T. S. Eliot." *Poetry Foundation*, Poetry Foundation, www.poetryfoundation.org/poetrymagazine/poems/44212/the-love-song-of-j-alfred-prufrock. Accessed 4 Dec. 2023.
20. Camus, Albert. *The Rebel*. Penguin Books, 2013.

8

The Art of Loneliness

When did I first encounter my solitude?

It's 4:50 in the morning and I'm waiting for my bus.

I don't want to romanticize a situation or shy away from the fact that my life has been largely that of privilege. This is the second time in my life I've ridden a public bus. Plenty of trains and subways, but only two bus rides. Well, that's not entirely true either. Regardless it is taking me where I am going. I've been movement. I've been stuck. As long as I am getting where I am going, then I am getting on.

As I place my coins in the slot for the fare and feel a tickle of enjoyment, I am forced to wonder why privileged America enjoys cosplaying as being poor? Myself included. Though I am no longer living off daddy's money (I am sure that is the narrative), but I will say this is the most I have ever made. I am not ahead by any means, but my dog's belly is full and I have a place to call my own. I love being a teacher.

The bus shakes from side to side as we cut through these southern streets. The driver is draped in darkness and I am drenched in phosphorescent light. Texting this document in my micro---cell phone. I have projects I am sitting on. Projects I'd like to receive what I have earned for them. Which outside of my time as a busker, I have received next to nothing for the works I have published. Though I am frequently gas lit into believing I am making no impact. This makes next to no real meaning to me. Knowing I effect one individual is enough for me. Of that notion I am certain. And the catharsis I receive from writing is payment in tenfold. Regarding my tumultuous hyperbolic emotional states, I am merely giving the listeners what they want. Perhaps, what they don't know they want.

Someone I was speaking to recently asked (regarding public speaking), "What if everyone starts laughing at you?". Well, then I have provided joy for a world desperate to feel. Feel anything for that matter.

We live in a time that is brutally self-aware of our species existential crisis. We have found the edges of our island, and there aren't enough resources to go around. Fear has turned us all into radicals. There is no side in the modern American political landscape that can feel comfortable about the division that exists in this country, all the while warfare and violence run rampant around the world. The debacle that has been our two previous presidents has led us to distrust not only our leaders, but our news sources. One could make the argument that your options are to be misinformed or uninformed. Many of us choose not to choose leading us into algorithmic hypnosis. In my moments of alienation or a desperate need for a dopamine fix, I too have relied on my feed for stimulating headlines, clips, or advertisements disguised as influencers and memes.

Presumably, I am still alive. Though I have my fair share of attempts to be unalive. Oddly enough, these aren't attempts that I have made as a result of solitude. I have only tried to kill myself when I have spent excessive amounts of time with the people who have raised me. When I have felt restrictions or ridicule toward my ability to think freely.

When I am alone—I am my best self. Occupying a certain level of self-assurance that I cannot offer in the presence of others. If only I could be so confident. There will come a time in my story where perhaps such confidence was embodied but for the large part it was done so under the guise of lies and betrayal. The freedom I have known has been manufactured. A question for another essay is: does that make freedom inauthentic? Is authenticity required in order for it be great?

How can I talk to you about the art of loneliness if I do not define loneliness. When I give it a search on the internet, the results I receive are along the lines of "no company", "solitary", or "a state of mind". These feel like a good lead, but I believe I am after something more philosophical. What I am about to write is pure abstraction. An attempt to grasp my thoughts on this experience that feels fundamentally human. It transcends time and culture. It is just as human as the desire to know the unknown, freedom, love, and hope.

I have come to conceive of sorrow as something along the lines of having the capacity or the memory of joy, while presently experiencing the lack of it. Or the inability to experience it. If we could make the claim that loneliness is a sorrowful experience, which I think is fair to say, then I'd like to take the framework of that definition and apply it to loneliness. This could look like, loneliness is the capacity or the memory of being whole, in community, and/or embraced by something bigger than yourself, while presently experiencing the lack of it. Or the inability to experience it.

What is that? When one cannot experience a very human experience. Joy, being whole, in community, or embraced by something bigger. You wear one of the many faces of humanity. Why do you see a stranger in the mirror? Why do we fear the citrus of possibilities in a garden of lovers and friends? At one point something happens to some of us where we prioritize safety over prosperity. I wonder if we have forgotten that one day we will die or that we cannot forget.

Anyways, about three months into living together it became clear that it wasn't going to last. We even had conversations about how we weren't the right fit, but we were staying together. Staying together out of obligations. Staying together out of necessity. One time she told me that she wanted to stay with me because she believed I'd be someone someday. Turns out I was someone then, but I didn't see that until now.

I don't care to flesh out the ugliness of that relationship, we were teenagers and then our erly twenties. We know nothing about everything and believed the opposite.

Rather I'll tell you aspects of my ugly and allow your imagination to make up the difference. The worst thing I ever did to her was, she took my truck to "hang out with friends", and she left me on the side of a snowy road around February of 2019. I owned a truck. She was using it. All I asked was that she pick me up from work. It was late. And the snow had mounted. Of course, I wasn't wearing boots. When I finally facetimed, her she was in somebody else's bed. After walking home with wet and frozen feet, I beat myself. I grabbed a frying pan and left my ribs black and blue.

Partially because I have a history of self-mutilation and I was in the spirit of deserving pain. Partially because I wanted to make her feel how shitty she made me feel. Not only did I give her my trust, but I gave her my fucking truck! So once my ribs were nice and bruised I told her I was victim of a hit and run. That some asshole hit me when I was crossing the street. That it would have never happened if she just did what she said she was going to do. To others I made up a lie and said she beat me with a frying pan in my sleep because she had a dream I was cheating. This was believable for a variety of reasons. She was an outwardly violent person and had laid hands on me before. Two, she was bat shit coocoo ka chew insane. It was part of the reason I loved her so deeply. Her crazy made me feel like mine wasn't that bad. But she was also hilarious. She didn't back down from anyone. When we were on the same page we could speak for hours. We were just struggling to get on the same page.

We were both controlling and this is the single instance of guilt I feel. I took our dynamic of manipulation too far. It revealed something terribly ugly about myself that would take a lot of work to understand and forgive.

I have just as many fond memories as bad ones, but really unpleasant ones about how are uglies complimented one another. We went to Rolling Loud together. We went to Costa Rica together. She really got me into weed and for that I have regrets. Make no mistakes I love that good old plant, but for all that it has given me it has taken as well.

Anyways, my reading habit at this point of my life has transitioned from audiobooks while working construction to making time to read with either a joint or a drink in tow. When she left sometimes both. A smoke followed up with a chilled red wine is a poisonous love. She goes to Miami with her girls and I get suspicious. I violate her trust, but for all intents and purposes the soundness of our trust had long been broken. I go into her laptop and see she had been meeting up with a guy from her past.

I was devastated and of all the people to read I was reading fucking Peterson. I remember writing in the margins of one of the twelve rules, "I hope nobody treats her the way she treats me.". When she gets back I end things.

I told her I was struggling with my sexuality. We had broken up more times than I could count. This felt like a sure-fire way to make sure she was gone for good. But this has also been a reoccurring theme through many relationships. See I have commitment issues and they express themselves as insecurities in identity. Since I was taught next to no copping skills other than compartmentalization and rage, this sentiment of weakness could only be one thing---I must be gay. For the most part I am just insecure. I have attempted to explore this facet of my identity, but there are some serious blocks as result of my past and my current relationship with trust. One day, I'll try to make it, make sense. For now, I gotta keep my head down and confide myself to abstraction. Just know that if I am a good man it is because I was once a bad one. Or at least one who made mistakes. I have been learning and improving. My light will shine rays on to what is going on in the shadows of others, those people will never let the world forget who I was. I will continue to offer who I have become.

See a flawed individual when you see me if you'd like. I see the face of redemption.

Anyways, when she left I went to Spain with my friends. If I am an ignorant of the world (which I am) now, then I was even more naïve all those years ago. When we went to Spain it was sort of exactly what I needed to not pay attention to the heart break I was definitely feeling.

I got to work. I'll keep writing when I get home later today.

There are a few points I want to talk about. Besides the parties, concerts, and getting inspired to write a story while basking in that northern Spanish sun. We took a train ride to Madrid. I knew the moment I saw this country that one day I'd like to live out there. I wish I prioritized that instead of the dreams of others. But I have to live with the decisions that I did and didn't make.

When in Madrid we went to that Museum. I saw the Garden of Earthly Delights by Bosch. Srgt. Pepper was adamant about seeing it. Raphael could have lived without it. Ahab was compromising. Rick couldn't be bothered. He was with us but his heart was in New Jersey. Alonso was in a balancing act of love and pleasure. He was trapped in a perpetual state of post-cum euphoria. We were looking at paintings, but he was trapped in the memory of love making.

All of our perspectives were suspended as we crowded around the painting. It was expansive and had a similar effect on the viewer.

Though I was undeniably changed by this, the moment of greatest significance at this museum was when I saw a painting of a Saint being crowned by a bird. I forget the name of the painting, but know it was just the name of this Saint. All I know is that in the description it said that this was the only painting in which the painter included a person. His other works are only landscapes. This was my first informal introduction toward a notion of transcendentalism.

I had developed the habit of meditation, but was long out of practice as a result of my relationship. My cup of bliss was filled by her kiss. So corny. What I know is that when I become involved with other people I tend to neglect the things I am passionate about.

When I got back to Syracuse my heart break was waiting for me and so were prints of some of the paintings that impacted me. As I hung them in my cockroach infested apartment I realized that this was the first art museum I had ever been to. Despite the fact that any chance I was given internet access or pen and paper I was engaging with something creative.

This is when a lifetime's worth of loneliness came to the surface. For in my solitude my misery had room to breathe. A man has never been known to sulk more than I did. I would go to work or class, just to return to the bottle or a smoke. Once I was about two-three chapters in is when I would begin to consume.

Whiskey and Dostoyevsky is a fascinating combination. Also, really enjoying Notes From the Underground is a very bad reason to make your email password Russia69!. Learn from my mistakes.

Anyways, I frequently use my history with mental health as a crutch or an excuse to not have faith in a higher power. See I didn't need God either way. I was living on my own, miserably on my own, but not being dependent on the people who raised me meant that maybe one day they will respect me.

See what happens next in my story is the truest and greatest source of my loneliness. My habit of meditating had picked up. My circumstances were alienating, but I was recognizing a specific sensitivity developing. Not sensitive like my feelings were being hurt more easily, but responsive to the pristineness of my senses.

So, I was pushing it, reading what I could and just being still. Trusting that if I sat in a certain position for long enough something would happen. One day something did.

Is this about loneliness or miracles? Sometimes I like to think that our ability to feel alone within ourselves is the greates gift of being. Oddly enough. If we didn't have this capacity to feel isolated would we even bother coming together?

Right, loneliness. We defined loneliness as the capacity to experience or the memory of wholeness and community, while simultaneously having the inability to experience it.

See one random afternoon I was mediating and felt the full fluidity of being, but as a result of the gates breaking open I experienced repressed memories of sexual abuse.

Repressed memories are a complicated thing. They tend to be revealing, but at the same time they damage your ability to trust what you know. Because I can only conceive of true knowledge (though others will make compelling arguments against or in addition to, but for as far as I am concerned I'd like to comment on this specific aspect of knowledge) can only be derived from experience. Or the memory of experiences. Having repressed memories subjugates all to doubt, while simultaneously creating two narratives of identity within the self.

Ergo, the birth of ruben.

There seems to be a "Master Self", which dictates the version of "me" allowed to drive the vehicle of my being. This is the state of being after almost five years of work and therapy that proceeds the experience being described.

At one of the most traumatizing points of my childhood, the man I admired most had his identity stolen over forty times. It seems somewhat logical that if there is any issue I struggle with, it is my sense of self.

But I had this experience of profound euphoria. I wanted nothing greater than to experience it, again and again and again. I wanted to remain there. Anywhere but there would not suffice.

Despite my efforts through meditation to repeat this spellbound experience, I no longer trusted myself. I had been forming a clay vase and this notion of doubt had been the crack that lets the water out.

See these memories of repressed sexual abuse, came to me in the form of infliction. I remember details about the act. I remember details about the pain. I remember details about telling myself, "if you don't think about it then it didn't happen.", as I cried myself to sleep. But what I couldn't seem to remember were the faces of the perpetrators. As I have gotten older, and pursued truth more details have come to me. Nevertheless, the details are always fragmented. Sometimes I remember who and the location, but the memories of the event are blacked out. Sometimes I remember the event and the location, but I don't remember who. All I truly know is that I have been lied to extensively and that anytime I get close to revealing the truth I am threatened. Either myself directly or the people I care for. It is unclear who, but I have begun to develop categories in my mind.

So here I am with many memories. Memories of the narrative of how I arrived at that moment. Memories that obscure the narrative in which I have formed my identity. Memories of the greatest and most abundant euphoria I have ever known. As a result of the contradictions in the first two I cannot experience the third. As a result of the first two I cannot trust community. The community that could help me confirm or deny what I had been through. I didn't choose it. I was a wolf among wolves, but I had to deviate. Even when I was with others I was alone.

This is the recipe of my sorrow. To know great joy, while simultaneously having the inability to engage with it. This is the recipe of my loneliness. To know what it is like to be amidst community (the past I knew was filled with people that I could not identify as someone who did or didn't inflict harm upon me) or to engage with something bigger than yourself (in this moment of bliss I felt as though I was nothing short of the universe experiencing itself), while simultaneously having the inability to experience it.

The months that followed I could only define my behavior as that of a functioning alcoholic. Though I never self-identify as an alcoholic because when it came time to stop, I just stopped. What was happening was more akin to a person desperate for solutions and company; alcohol just produced more consistent feelings than people did.

I would tutor some of my classmates in exchange for coffee and books. One day I bought a journal for the first time since my ex had left. I tried writing things narratively, but all that came out was broken verse.

It was here where I truly began to contemplate that perhaps our response to loneliness was the determinant toward the quality in which we used to live. I was engaging in a variety of texts, but the writings of the stoics were particularly resonating. I have revisited the works of stoic philosophers with caution throughout the years. I say with caution because though I find their teachings to be insightful, I must also acknowledge the pitfalls of stoic teachings. A pitfall that I had engaged with as I wrestled with the desire to be the strength of masculinity while simultaneously being immersed in the wonder that is femininity.

See stoicism can quickly be radicalized into repressing emotions that bear the credence to be felt. As a result of this traumatizing and enlightening moment of awakening, one thing became clear to me. Perhaps not in an intellectual sense, but in a spiritual and embodied way. I can only articulate this because once my sulking ended I wanted answers and began studying more intentionally. As opposed to following my curiosity as to where it led me.

The confines of binary gender norms are not the way the self comes to actualize. Actualization, for me in simplistic terms, is allowing yourself to occupy the potential of beauty you contain within the vastness of all your experiences and all the experiences to come. To be a universe experiencing itself, while acknowledging that you are nothing more than stardust. A poet is a paradox with linguistic abilities who chooses to use those abilities expressively in dedication to something greater. I am certain I will define what it means to be a poet differently, for I am a poet and I must contradict myself.

As a result of consistently cultivating the ideals of masculinity within me I long neglected the "ignorant girl" within me. Ignorant for she lacks the world's experience that he has. Girl instead of woman because she has remained stuck in the second grade, my earliest memory of sexual abuse. From that moment forward to allow such wonderous femininity to arise to the surface was an indicator of weakness when it should have been an indicator of beauty.

But at the time I was a whiskey drinking stoic. Working hard, physically isolated, and a lonely soul. This is how I lived for a year, and as a response to this year I have only developed upon the foundations that were built during this time.

Work or school upon alternating days. On the weeks I'd get paid two bottles of Jack Daniels. On the weeks I didn't get paid, four bottles of wine. An eighth of weed about every week to ten days. A book a week. I only went out to bars or parties a handful of times. It was three times in a year and a half.

What has changed since then is I don't I drink as often. The nature of my work is different. I have two bachelor's degrees. My crafts have improved. My apartment is bigger, better, and has nicer view. There aren't cockroaches but I a bit like one. I have got a dog. The best dog. A man could not ask for a better dog. She is more loyal than the loneliness that emowers me.

The ideas were in the oven back then, but we are fully baked now. What my solitude taught me was that, if you cannot find community amongst others, learn to be community within yourself. Allow every variation of you were, within the journey of you are becoming who you are, to be greater than fragmented memories. Allow the multiplicity of the self to become kin. I have become a father to the neglected child of my past. I have become friends with the misunderstood weirdo. I have become the sponsor to the self-destructive alcoholic. I have become the big brother to misunderstood and insecure artist. I have become a mother the heart broken and confused girl.

This is the art of loneliness. To take this solitary state and fill it with experience. Allow this experience to serve as the variety of color. The moral integrity of your decisions to be the movement of brush strokes, as they come together and form the painting upon the canvas of your existence.

What will emerge is a vision that only you can comprehend. And you must only listen to the judgment of those who were present for your solitude (the multiplicity of self) as to whether that vision is worth breathing life into. Everything and everyone else are just noise. Always trust love. It's going to hurt you. It will also make you.

The arts are subjective. There is no good or bad, just decisions and emotion. Never pass judgment on what you are creating for yourself.

More often than not your body knows what it is trying to reveal to you. You will only grasp the artform of your existence in retrospect.

There is much I can say about my time in Syracuse. But the characteristic that marks it the most is my loneliness. What I truly know since then is that I have no conception of how I arrived where I arrived. What I do know is that I went back home and shook things up. What I do know is I accomplished my goals. What I do know is that I write to you from the south. In the land of Faulkner, Appalachia, and blue grass. What I know is used to be alone and I hated myself. What I know is I am alone and I am proud of who I am becoming.

Poetry has been my brushstrokes. What you are about to read are when I began to paint. What you are about to read are poems from my time in Syracuse. From my desolation. What you are about to read is when I began to reclaim my loneliness, and turned into art.

With a sweaty back and filled lungs,
ruben encontrado

the pseudonym of Ruben De Escapado

9

What is Hope?

I have to be careful not to rush this. This idea of hope. It is the most important part of the human experience to my life itself.

Esperanza. I love the word in spanish. I am sure some of you know that. But hope in english is so declerative. Whereas in spanish the word rolls off the tongue with a sense of longing. To put my sentiment simply that is what hope is. An intense yearing.

I suppose that is the question more than what hope is specifically. What do we yearn for?

Growing up I quickly became aware of my limitations. The limitations in agency of childhood. Not being trusted with some responsibilities and trusted with others. The limitations in ability. Seeing older kids lift heavier weights, do more complicated math, smoking cigerrettes, drinking alcohol, and driving places.

But then there was deeper, less identifiable limitations. The school I went to growing up was odd in the sense that it was perhaps preparing us for the world to come and not the world that is. I suppose all good schools do this. The Catholic school I went to gave special priviledges to the girls while the boys were punished at every turn. So there were the limitations of my gender. Not only in immediate priviledge, but in a larger social sense. How you dress and how you are expected to behave in your boyhood years. I am in no way making the comparison that men have it more difficult then women. What I am saying is that my cock and balls did not gaurantee me an easy life. Though I am sure it was easier than some. Probably more difficult than some as well. What I am highlighting are limitations.

Another limitation in my upbringing was my name. Nobody said it right and I was never encouraged to correct others. From the outside I heard the bleached verision of my namesake and within I heard the R's rolling. I went to a predominantly white Irish Catholic elementary school. My parents grew up in a time where it was best that people didn't know you were an immigrant. This false sense of passing had them raising me and my brothers as if we were the *special* kind of hispanic/latino. What this life with all of it's limitations will quickly teach you is that nobody and I mean absolutely nobody is special. What makes us common is the unique ways in which we are all exceptional.

It was at this Catholic School where I made some of the best friends a man could ask for. Had some of the richest and most nurishing experiences possible. It was also the place where I experienced sexual abuse. An experience that I think I speak about to lightly for the comfort of others. I don't care to seak about in depth not because it didn't happen, but because there is more to my story then childhood trauma. But I must mention it now because I because my struggle to manage this experience and mature in a traditional way feels like it is seemingly a result of my identity.

My boyhood turned my manhood. My ethnicity and my journeys through enviorments in which it is hated, disregarded, and celebrated. It wasn't until I went to a public high school that I learned to take pride in my last name and my heritage. Suddenly the otherness that I had grown accustomed to was celebrated. I saw my flag in the hallway everyday as I walked to the cafeteria.

Then I worked construction for many years and amidst immigrant workers I spoke in my native tongue everyday for five years. Forty hours a week of rhythmo and tambor. When I reflect on this time I can't tell if I miss working with my hands or conversing in Spanish everyday.

But there were limitations to a public high school. The same way there was limitations in working constructions. So, I went to community college and things were getting better, but there were limitations there. Then I went to a private college and there were limitiations there. Then I began to dedicate myself to my spiritual practice and there were limitations to *this*. This body.

What if I told you I believe we are more internal than external? What if I told you I have believed this since boyhood? Struggling with the demands of masculinity. The same masculinity that was limiting my voice as I attempted to advocate for myself. Advocating within the confines of not being heard and incongruency of communicating that occurs as a response to trauma while one's consciousness developing. Consciouness, from my persepctive, being the mere linguistic organization of memories in some order. The less traumatized you are the more chronological and linear. The more traumatized the more fractured.

Not only did I recognize that we were more internal than external, but my internal---as a result of pain and the varying limitations of existening---was crumbling. I was a hurting child trying to communicate danger, pain, and confusion to adults in a language of my own. Another limitation. You say "Table". An image comes to your head. A different but similar image comes to mine. The way we converse is different but similar enough so that we can function. But nobody. Absolutely nobody on this planet will see things exactly how you see things. Not even a twin.

And so we try. To go beyond these limitations because each one of us has our own set of unfoldings. Occuring in each and every moment of conscious life. Perhaps that is what the yearning is. At least that's perhaps what it is to me. To have my specific fragmentation make sense to at least one other person. For perhaps if they can see things how I see things, then what I see might come together. Come together in a way in which this fight to perserve this tangible limited and decaying body feels more worth allowing the wonderous internal prism of glow exist without limitations.

Is that what hope is? This pursuit to find meaning in the maintance in the body that feels like the agent of suffering and limitations. When the possibility of a limitless dreamscape lives within us like a fountain that cannot be seen, but felt.

In my previous essay I talked about how the all pervasive human desire was an encompassing fear of dying. That this is the true will of decision. The preservation of life as a result of not wanting to enter the great unknown.

Though I do find the research in that project and the argument made is a strong one, there are comments I want to make to that point.

If fear is the all pervasive force that controls our decisions, the only way to truly ascertain freedom. To live authetically. You have two choices to live with free will. You can be spiteful. Or you can be compassionate. An agent of anger and hatred. An agent of love and charity.

Any other way of being does not cause any real change. Change is the causal evidence of freedom. I choose love and charity. Not because it is inherently better though I am sure I could make the argument that it is. I choose to be an agent of love and charity because it is the more difficult route. It is more difficult to validate then anger and hatred. And because it is more difficult I know it is the route in which my life will be more meaningful.

I'll write an essay on what love is or looks like one day.

The second comment I'd like to make to that point is that when I was going to kill myself, I didn't go through with it because of a fear of dying. I didn't go through with it because of something else. If I had to theorize an explanation from a scientific perspective then the only thing that would seemingly make sense is that as I was about to plunge myself with the dagger my brain must have released DMT. I can only theorize such an explantion in retrospect and in order to explain what I had gone through.

I must refernce these ten seconds in which my story was supposed to end with a period, but instead some grand author decided to put a semi colon.

That semi colon was the most important ten seconds of my life. For in those ten seconds of color and shapes and deep sound and mesmerizing frequencies and still movement something far greater than anything I had previously experienced occured. The mantra of my existence transitioned from *why not* to *I must*. In that moment of meaningless I saught meaning in my destruction, but I found reason in my preservation. A reason that went far beyond any limitation that had ever inhibitted me.

Now as my life circumstances progressively unfold at the hands of advantegous people, self destructive interpersonal skills, and absolutely no prospects outside of a seemingly profitless writing carreer the limitations of my life carry no weight. The weight I now carry is the reason that goes beyond my limitations. This all pervasive feeling of *I must continue forward*. Somedays I think the obligation is toward a verision of me that doesn't exist yet. Most of the time I feel as though it is toward a generation of children who have not arrived on this planet yet. If I don't make my voice and persepctive heard will the signs of my trauma also go unrecognized in the becoming of someone else's boyhood. If I don't find ways to take pride in my ethnicity and sense of identity, then who else will think it is okay to not allow their vibrancy to shine bright.

I try not to write in the lens of belief toward a higher power though I beleive there is some great cosmic force that connects us all. A chunk of the universe given to us at birth that we must return at death. I try not write from that lens because for many this world is godless. We gotta find a way to go beyond our limitations without a higher power for the sake of those who have been let down by this universe.

So I suspend my beliefs directly in my work and in my conversation. Whether those are religious, political, or business beliefs. In the attempt to make my message universal. I am not interested in telling people what their destination ought to be. I am interested in getting people on the train. For as the Indian Proverb states, "Sometimes the wrong train gets you to the right destination.".

What is hope? I have expressed some thoughts, but I am not sure I can identify something so intangible. If there is a soul, then I think we can equate it to the sentiment of hope. So perhaps hope is the memory of being full in the moments in which we are empty. The drive to return to the moment of wholeness for we know that it is out there. Just beyond the limitations of our present moment.

That's hope to me. Or at least what it is at this present moment. It's the closest thing to an explantion that I can come up with as to why I continue when the limitations of my life communicate to me continously to stop.

10

What is Freedom?

At the time in which I wrote the poems you are about to read, I would have assumed myself to be the authority on this subject. This assumption being made under the premonition that I had ascertained something akin to an absolute freedom. Now as I reflect on this lick almost two years after deciding to close the door on my Central Busker life, I cannot help to feel like I have never truly known what freedom is.

This essay is not research based. I am merely entertaining abstraction and being deconstructive in my methodology. Please, at no point should you approach my work as an extension or an attack on any beliefs that you have. I am merely working out my thoughts. If they provide perspective for you as well, all the better.

I suppose there are a few questions I must address:

1. What is freedom?
2. What is absolute freedom?
3. Have I ever been free?
    a. The reason I ask this question is when I reflect on the narrative of my life I have been ignorantly powerless to external forces. So perhaps a way to extend this question would be, what is the relationship between power and freedom?

A short answer to the first question, what is freedom, is the ability to make choices. This feels somewhat short sighted. See if I have considered this a number of times while walking my dog. She sniffs flowers to the right. She pees on a bush to the left. Side to side to side. Freely choosing where she goes, but ultimately it is I who am in control.

She is surely making choices, but when I am the one who decides when it is time to go back home, to the park, to play fetch, or to go down one street instead of another.

Perhaps, the knowing being can never have the sense of illusory joy that a dog might indulge in as a result of their ignorance. I say ignorance not because dogs aren't brilliant creatures, in fact I am of the position that they are far more intelligent than humans, but for the reason that their consciousness is not bound by the constraints of thinking linguistically. This human condition is our most exceptional and also our pitfall. Languages have tenses so we can conceive of past and future; dogs only know the presence. Rather they don't even know they just are. Languages have structures which bind us to logic and reason; dogs only know desires. Or intuition. Or some combination of both. I am hypothesizing possibilities. I know next to nothing on animal consciousness.

I remember when I was in Catholic School, going to mass on Wednesdays. When I got a bit older I would be an alter boy, but the moment I am about to refer to was from before that. Many things confused me about my experience in Catholic School. I have unknowingly been pushed in a very specific direction by my parents. Both have had independent and conflicting agendas towards the trajectory of my life. I refuse both.

I mention my confusion because I believe that it is the immersion into this confusion accompanied with the retreated mysteriousness of my father that first sparked the interest of my philosophical inquiry.

I remember being in Church, completely disassociating from the monsignor's homily, and wondering how did Jesus know he was the son of God. I knew that it was prophesized and he received whatever signs he had received, but I couldn't help to entertain the idea of what consists of making a sign a "sign". What if the sign is that he were the son of god, was merely the thought coming to him out of the blue? The way so many of my thoughts had frequented my passing pondering. Instead of it being a silly thought, he chose to believe it. What if that was all it took to know that you were the child of God? Merely to believe in the notion so deeply that it was as if it were a knowing. Again, this is the structure of my boyhood thoughts.

This concerned me deeply. I was very distracted from my classes. Exploring abstraction frequently draws my attention away from learning facts. All it takes is a small data point to give me the idea for a critique, argument, dilemma, character, poem, or narrative and before you know it the imagery in my head has veiled visuals of my surroundings.

At some point, I had to get to the bottom of things. I had confessed somewhat recently, but I knew it was the only way I'd be able to speak to the priests individually. Or at least in a way that was worthwhile.

I was hesitant because the last time I had done confession I had admitted to watching porn. At this point in my prebusence I knew of porn and porn sites, but I didn't understand the concept of masturbating. Nor do I think I had the capacity to ejaculate had I tried. This was merely of habit of entertainment, trying to understand what adults did, and complicating the nature of pleasure for the adult me. I will admit my erection pressing into my spandex before soccer practice felt good enough to continue the habit.

I reminded myself that I had said my ten Hail Mary's and that god had forgiven me. I could speak to the priest with a clear conscious. Well as clear as a child with a conception of original sin's consciousness can be.

I stepped into that dark closet space. "Bless me father for I have sinned, it has been three weeks since my last confession.", "What is it my child? You can tell me anything.". "How do I know God is real?".

From a young age freedom seemed like a very important thing to me. Not freedom, the ability to make choices. I was choosing to watch porn when I could. Experimenting with how many additional seconds cooked my hot pocket to perfection. No, I was born with an immense longing for something greater. Something so deeply profound. Some days I think it might be the yearning to be aligned with desire. Just an unrestrained existence. But a part of me knows that since I can remember what I identified as the longing freedom went a layer deeper. Now as an adult having learned so much about what was kept from me, I have come to understand that what I really craved was to belong.

Some time has passed since I last opened this document. Not a long time, but not a short time either. I hear my voice in the words above, but they are merely an echo of who I was. Grown is the word. I am on my way to NY. I have burned more bridges than I can count. In their ashes I hope I have built a few as well.

I am heading to NY. I am two months late on rent. A third is about to be due and I have $437 dollars and a typewriter to my name. The illusion of freedom amidst all of my restrictions has made me a gambling man. Some might even say an outlaw. Since last visiting this document, I have self-published two projects. I have gotten into a fight and been arrested. Spent a night in solitary. Bought a motorcycle. Immortalized the motorcycle, a white Honda rebel 500, through speed and tenacity. It is now known as the comet. I am known as many things. I am known for getting things done.

But what is freedom now that I have been fighting for it and for others. I think a few months ago when I started writing this, I would have given you an answer like freedom is the agency and the ability to choose what we do. This is not wrong. But what I come to understand now is that freedom is a fight. An all-pervasive fight in which we cannot submit our thinking to the patterns of our society. For despite the structure, organization, and legislation in which the world operates upon; the individual is the agent of order. It is the masses and the constructed extensions of the masses in which chaos does reside.

This may feel counterintuitive for we have always viewed nature as some sort of aesthetic representation of chaos. But the chaos we see is reactionary in the pursuit of equilibrium. Nature wants balance. It doesn't want it demands. And so, when things become too orderly, we see the destruction of all that is imposed upon us. Perhaps this is the decay of free will.

And so the only way to truly ascertain a notion such as free will we must resist the conformity that is imposed upon us. Or the conformity in which we impose upon ourselves. I think it is important to always focus on building the megaphone before you speak out. But in the wise words of Borges, "Speak only if you can improve the silence.".

My biggest fear as my voice begins to develop is that I begin to speak over others. Random thought---I'll continue.

How are you counterculture to the very culture of your psyche? I wish I had a step by step. Mental health issues can be your best friend in this pursuit. Or it could be the thing that leans you into the habits you have developed? There isn't exactly a recipe. You are just throwing spices into the pan. Taking a tablespoon as the meal heats up. A splash of this. A pinch of that. You set out to make Chicken Picata and suddenly you have a Pornstar Margaritas. Such is life.

I think the very first step must be solitude. You have to spend copious amounts of time alone to truly know who you are. The second thing has to be created. No matter what that looks like. Painting, music, writing, knitting, sculpting, Legos, or whatever. Let the only conditions of your creations be the pursuit of curiosity in a judgment free way.

In each moment there is the opportunity to sell ourselves short. In that sense our body is own worst enemy. It is the mind that must rise above the temptation to be less than who we are. This is the only habit I recommend. This and regular sex if you can. I am better at the former than the latter. Such is life.

I think if you do these things enough then the currents you will naturally emit will be counter intuitive to your surroundings. Some people gravitate to those who play the game of life well. The struggles. The ups and downs. The big decisions and the game day ones. Others gravitate to those who change the way it is played. An argument for freedom could be made for both.

As I ride this flight. Disconnected exterior influence for the first time in months. I am left wondering which way is better. If that's even a question worth asking. It may very from each individual. I used to say make the decision that allows for empathy to be what you are aligned with. This may be the start to something bigger. Where empathy, towards oneself and towards others, is tends to lead is to a profound authenticity. A declerative presence in the universe. One that states *I am here* wherever you go.

The path that I have chosen to walk is one of great suffering. But as I sit with cold toes, looking I down on a foggy evening sky, I am nostalgic of the winter days in Central Park, in which I wore the same boots that I wear today. I was filled with wonder then and I am filled with experience now. Ironically enough both versions of me are tireless, fascinated, and optimistic. Though I wear darker colors now.

Freedom is an illusion if it does not include all. And so if freedom is what you pursue not comfort, then get off your ass. Find something worth fighting for and surrender to the struggle when you are dead. Never compromise your morals. Lose if winning means stooping to the level of others. And never ever lose hope. Freedom for all is what we strive for and hope is what keeps whole thing together when everything around us tells us we should be broken.

I have just edited this essay after not looking at it in what feels like a lifetime. I brought up my catholic school upbringing in correlation to freedom, but never expressed why. It was on those fields at recess.

It was in the cafeteria in friends. In the gym. After school. In which my catholic experience is as wonderous as my classmates remember it to be. I don't know if I would trade how wonderful my child hood was with anyones. But there are these moments. In which I could have just forgetten. In fact, I had forgotten. But then they came back to me. For a long time I couldn't hold myself. But then my chest was filled. My shoulders felt broad, again. I used to think if I can fuction with having gone through the trauma of the event, but if I could have gone through the grief of rewriting all of my memories and still found ways to endulge in forgiveness. Rise up and be a bigger human being. Hoping my paths will not cross with those of my past. Then I will be a good little cog in the machine of exterior big city suburbia.

But then I found something I loved doing. I loved it more than anyone could. It's a wonderous thing to share tears with a stranger. And that felt compromised. I no longer felt safe and the cause felt justifiable enough were I felt like a different approach to my artitic endevors needed to happen. I had to scramble the memory of who I was. Not my own, but I had to make people forget who I was.

It wasn't something I wanted, but if I disapeared. It would give me the opportunity to grow stronger. Figure out what was going on. And hopefully undo much of the trauma that I was experiencing.

The only problem was it wasn't an act. I wanted to disappear disappear. The greatest way to escape this world was to escape it completely. When in that instant I did not go through with my own destruction I found a deep fight living within me. I have told myself repeatedly that the moment in which I chose to live was the moment I found hope. But the truth is it's when I found fight. Where I found grit. It was then and only then when I was deep in the North Carolina woods. That I knew I needed to defend myself. That I could no longer keep trying to escape the trauma of my past. My tent was beneath a tarp. I had a small fire burning at the mouth of the tipi. It rained for three days. I read Basho.

I was in the deepest stage of contemplation I had ever been in. I met a woman and her daughter living on the campgrounds. What they represented made me fall in love deeply with a life perhaps forgotten by others but remembered by the trees.

I felt like if I didn't let fear get the better of me, she would have let me stay with her for as long as I would have liked. But fear did get the better of me. For the trauma I was struggling to manage was deeply rooted in Biblical stories that were taught to us out of order.

What I have never quite expressed to anyone as I saw this opportunity to live the life I wanted, I felt like I needed to run. For a long time I could not forgive myself for my supposed fear. But the more deeply I contemplated, the more aparent it became that I needed to fight back. Because if I did anything other than that, then it would never end.

That and as I mentioned befor the intergration of my trauma and biblical stories being expressed in my mania. From a very young age it feels like I have been conditioned to either be the marytr second coming or the social revolutionary that would restore balance to the burning America. Americassss. The United States is the country club of the Americas. Our latin neighbors to the south suffer more often then not by how rich our economey became at the expense of our dollar against theirs. The moments leading up to my attempt were difficult to describe. But when I was in the woods. I began to entertain an extremely confusing thought. Perhaps, I should abandon my dog.

Release my dog into the woods. Or maybe I shouldn't even allow it to suffer. Maybe I should kill my dog. Then once I have done that I should kill myself. If you know me then you know how important my dog is to me. She is the best friend I have ever had in my life. No disrespect to the great people I have gotten to know. I go everywhere with her if I can.

The mere fact that I would even entertain such a thought made me feel like I could not even attempt to stay with this small family of peace. I needed to keep moving. I needed to go somewhere warmer. I needed to out run my demons. And so I drove as fast as I could. Listening to different music as loud as it went. All the while turning over these thoughts about the intergration of my life story and the biblical ones. Because the more I thought about this desire to leave my dog behind the more it felt like I was compelled to. The more I questioned what it meant to be compelled to do something. The more I thought about the story of Abraham and Isaac.

This was particularly revealing when I read Kierkegaard a year later and he entertained various ways in which that story could have played out. While reading this book I contemplated the memories of this event deeply.

See the internalization of these memories and the internaliation of biblical stoires being inflicted upon me occurred in the same sequence of events.

For a long time the source of the wound couldn't be identified. But then I remembered something one day. It was just the sink. I remembered the white framing around the window. I remembered the steel sink. The cabinets to the left and right of the window. That the window looked down at the park the students would go to recess to. I remembered that I was alone. Or at least not with a family member. The only thing I could think after that is why was I in that house at all. Suddenly, I remembered moments from my life in which I was asking classmates if they had ever been inside that house.

Before all of this had even occurred a priest from my past had grabbed my ass.

I was beginning to piece things together, but I still didn't know who. Then after a great deal of suffering, I see this guy. He has a sign out in public the way I had a sign out in public. "Tell us your story", there are cameras set up all over the place. So, I sit with him. And I tell him what I vaguely remember going through.

See I had gottent tipped off that the peace I was after had been completely taken from me. That there was no chance the people who didn't want me talking about what they thought I knew would allow me a moment to breathe. Which I had finally arrived at a moment where I was catching my breath. My only choice without evidence was to turn on the spotlights. Expose their shadows and amidst their nuditiy someone else could corroborate my story.

As I continue to develop into who I am. I hope that by progressively revealing what I have been through allows for me approach my trauma in a way that is productive for my well being and for those involved in the sensitive moments that I am forced to relive in hopes that I will get peace and justice for what I was forced to endure.

And desite all the explaining I have done. I have not offered my position on any of the questions I initially asked. What is freedom? Maybe it was my initial response. The ability to make choices and go where one would freely wills themselves to. But this type of freedom is bound by the rights of our community. Laws protecting what can be done and what cannot be done for the sake of coehision and order.

Perhaps, there is our notion of absolute freedom. We long for it and immerse oursleves in the pursuit for it as we leave the brick and mortor to go hiking, camping, and hunting. Drawn in by the allure of nature as something more authentic to the reality in which we function daily. But even our notion of nature is from the scope of suburbia, city life, and even rural life. I ponder if the allure of nature or nature as art is merely the allure of a beastly existence. One in which the problems of abstraction never existed the puruit of Maslow's hierarchy is on the forefront of a waking reality.

I hate that I even entertain the idea that the sensitivity that we experience while immersed in nature isn't the something being heightened but the absence of something we have grown accustomed to. Something we have deemed worse because the experience itself is just different.

The inclination to identify this experiences as an absolute freedom is high. We think freedom and an image of a bird soaring through the sky comes to mind. It is when we are in the blissful silence of nature that a similar sensation euphoria soars within us. And yet I cannot help but feel that this is not the absolute freedom I am thinking of. I am unfortunately under the impression that the natural state of humanity is the potential for violence. That when left to our own devices more often than not, the lack of control we have over our own waking vulnerability (a vulnerability exposed to us by the knowledge that we will die one day), we yearn to assert control. Control in the form of violence more often than not. Unfortunately. And so though this notion of absolute freedom is enticing, it is also dangerous. Such a dangerous sensation that it can be convulded with the allusion of power. I say allusion because the only real power that there is exists within community. An individual being the agent of power merely has advantage over the advantagless.

Power being infinite and advantage being finite.

So, a notion such as freedom can be great, but a notion such as absolute freedom is dangerous. Unless the world becomes beat. For perhaps sex is a violent act. My only hesitation in proclaiming that what this world needs is a cosmic orgy, is that in a time in which ethically questionable acticity is occuring (heinous amounts of crime, violence, and warfare. Political agendas driven by gaining advantage throught the promotion of hate and ideological exclusion.), what becomes ethically permissable is increasingly grey.

I then I answer you the question, have I ever been free, and to that answer the simple response is no. In the moments, in which I laid claim to my own freedom another, more advantegous individual or entity, laid the stronger claim. Not because it was more logical or thoroughly articulated, but because they were significantly more well connected and better funded.

The credit card debt I accumulated in my early twentites have hovered over me throughout college, my art carreer, and as I tried to make my way into the world of education. My history of seeking help, restrengthening, and healing have been held against me as evidence of my incompetency and immaturity. Where through distance, challenging reframing, and the love of strangers I have deconstructed much of the structures that encaged me. The bars of my internal prison cell was the perception that my maturity and strength to seek help as I attempted to embody the ending of generation cycle have been embedded deep into me as evidence of my inadequacy. It has become abundantly clear to me that my greatest inadequacy is my habitualization of forgiving remorseless individuals.

My truth is destroying them. If you see me with heavy shoulders it is not because of the weight of my trauama. Or the countless rodeos that have gone documented and undocumented. The weight I carry now is the guilt of knowing how heavy my truth is. That the only way to relinquish myself of it's burden is for those who have distorted my perception of it to carry it's weight in a nakedness. I want everyone to know who might think the suffering of the individuals I have loved that have arguably done wrong by me may be justified that it is not. Suffering never is. We often seek to validate it through the belittling of anothers. As less authentic or not as great, but we all carry the weight.

I am seemingly a cry baby who feels like they need theirs to be heard. I have often entertained that the artist is trying to recreate a memory that they don't know they remember. I was told I was a collique baby. Perhaps I am just a collique man suffering from PTSD, confusion, and fear. The same fear we all carry, but aren't willing to admit there is. But I am a truth teller. Even if I am hated I must say and highlight the thing nobody is willing to. We all are afraid of what happens next. That's the easiest part. To acknoweldge how blatantly aware our generation is of our existensial situation. We are experiencing a global existential crisis. It's everywhere we go, slightly beneath the surface. Felt, but never acknowledged.

What runs just a layer beneath that is the way our communities have come together. Sure we have never lived in such tribal times, but the creed of friendship has never had such deep bonds. We live in a time where a stranger in a coffee shop would take a bullet for you because you told them they looked nice on a Thursday evening after a difficult day of work.

We just see news head lines of what is going wrong and social media algorithm's with a Machavelli complex. And so the wonderous love that lives slightly under the frequency of existential tension we all feel.

So, no I have never been free. For when I broke free from the shackles of my family's control, the burden of legacy was carried with me, and when I relinquished myself of my last name more people laid claim to the work that I have put in.

"Man is born free and everywhere in shackles.", this qoute from Rousseau comes from an essay I read in college that I do not care to reference properly. But the sentiment holds true to this idea that absolute freedom is this notion of boundlessness. Such a notion that this is the freedom we should strive for feels difficult for me to comprehend. Difficult because I prescribe to the idea that the natural state of humanity is the potential for violence. By allowing such an idea to be permissable can have two fold scenarios. The first being slipping into chaos. A world in which murder, rape, warfare, and genocide are social permissable ideas. The second is that we adopt the notion that sex is a violent act. We become superfolous lovers living lifestyles of pornstars and jigalows. I think there is a certain liberal idealogy that strives for an absolute freedom that I tend to agree with for the sake of inclusivity and progressiveness. The flip side of this notion is that such incistent inclusvity with a contradictory ridigness to a demographic of people who aren't inclusive may lead to the prospective scenario of chaos. Chaotic violence. The same could be said about the hyper conservative perspective that isn't as inclusive. Because no matter what the scenario is the inability to communicate and entertain ideas that you do not agree with will lead to a single mindedness in a community of many minds. I think what I would implore conservatives to entertain is do you think it is possible to keep things they are or were when time itself is the measurment of change through movement. I would implore more liberal thinking individuals to entertain is two things. Is everything from the past a bad thing? The second thing is when you place limitations on what can and can't be said is it easier or more difficult to gauge the character and beliefs of an individual? Perhaps, in the pursuit of validating everyone's truth you are undermining *the* truth. I think the same can be said to conservatives. Both sides are angry and when both sides are angry all that needs to be said what y'all want to hear. Y'all are screaming what you want to hear. Any dickhead with money can win you over. But you burry the few who try to say what you need to hear.

So, freedom outside of the perameters of basic human rights is something to be approached with caution. To the individual who self identifies as a cat shitting in a kitty litter somewhere on a college campus and the conservatist anarchist who is horny to point their rifle at someone who's skin tone doesn't look like the one they see in the mirror; I implore you to consider the same freedom you advocate for with different words in the hands of gang bangers, street kings, and organized crime that have a much stronger claim to be dishackled by the restrictions of our society. What I would like you to understand as well is that it is the viscious cycles of history that have undermined our constituion, but not our constitution itself. This seminal document is the greatest document of freedom and democracy that has ever been written. But it was written in a time whent the foundations of this country were being built by individuals interpreted the work advantegously.

To be an American, not documentation but national identity, is to seek belonging upon a land that was never yours. Unless you are amongst the indigenous community your claim to this land is no greater than any other strangers. The immigration story is the American story. I knew that growing up. I knew that while working with migrants workers. I understand that now as I am distant from all that I knew. Tell me there is something more American, but to strive for something better by going somewhere unfamiliar. The yearning for your coffee mug. The yearning for the way the bakery you never went into smelled like as you walked by. For the gas station clerk who always called you, "buddy.".

I have gotten distracted, but what I was trying to highlight is the increasing ethical grey area that comes with the pursuit of absolute freedom. The necessity to entertain ideas you disagree with. To find commanality. To ackoweldge that the constitution is not flawed, but human history is. A humany history that we have inherited.

We should lean into a notion of free love and oneness, but not with lines drawn. We must continue to read and write texts, engage with any medium of art that challenges how we have come to understand the world.

What I can tell you about a life in which I have largely been trapped. My spiritual, sexual, and political beliefs have been restricted since a young age. I remain to myself about these things because I prescribe to the belief that if I am doing the world of artistry correct. That if I am a voice amidst the voices then you will never know where I stand or what I do. The only belief that I will amdit so directly about the source of my ideology is that I am a humanitarian and a communtarian. Though I am critical of modern transcendentalism how I have chosen to engage with the world's wonder has made me a transcendentalist. This makes me no spokesperson or expert on these subject matters, but from what I have read about these works they offer the greatest explanation as to how I have chosen to approach this life.

None the less this approach has taken a great deal of work. Everything I have ever learned was actually just an unlearning of something I was misinformed on. I have never been free. Because once I liberated myself from my past I dedicated my servitude to something greater. Not towards any God. Not towards any belief. Not towards any cause. But to breathe life into a literary movement that will give hope to the next seven generations. A time frame that I predict the novel and our ecosystem will surely die off.

It was never about winning or being successful. It was about giving a surely hopeless generation that is to come the last sliver of lights there. Never give up. Even if it is futile. Especially when it is futile.

from the circus before the storm,
ruben

ruben encontrado is a self-published poet, author, painter, and photographer. He self identifies as delicious, happy, a bit odd, an activist, a hawk, and absolutely ridiculous.

His published works include Lame & Liminal and Metamorphosis. He has written the preface to works by Delta Okes. He is also in the editing process of an unnamed project. He thinks everyone should be better. As individuals and better off.